Chicken Cookbook

Elizabeth Pomeroy

HAMLYN
London · New York · Sydney · Toronto

Contents

Acknowledgements

The author and publishers thank the following
for their co-operation in supplying colour photographs
for this book:

Sun Valley Poultry Limited
Page 19:   Chicken in a basket
Page 27:   Raised game or chicken pie *and* Vols-au-vent
Page 59:   Paella a la Valenciana

Syndication International
Page 23:   Chicken and ham pie à la Russe, Welsh leek
        and chicken pie, Alsatian chicken and cheese tart
        and Chicken or game piroshki

Line drawings by Hayward Art Group

Published by
The Hamlyn Publishing Group Limited
London · New York · Sydney · Toronto
Astronaut House, Feltham, Middlesex, England
© Copyright 1973 The Hamlyn Publishing Group Limited

ISBN 0 600 31798 6
Text set in 'Monophoto' Univers by
London Filmsetters Limited
Printed by Chapel River Press Limited,
Andover, England

Introduction

There are so many delicious and diverse ways of cooking chicken that I found it very difficult to decide which to choose for this book.

What I have tried to do is, firstly, to help the beginner home cook with basic information and enjoyable uncomplicated recipes to overcome any initial lack of confidence and to embark on shopping and cooking with positive pleasure, instead of anxiety. Next, to encourage the more experienced cook/host and hostess to enliven their menus with some dashing new dishes which they will enjoy preparing and the guests have pleasure in eating. Incidentally, if you are calorie counting, grilled or roast chicken provides one of the most appetising meals for slimmers.

There are many home cooks for whom the demands of a job outside the home and/or a lively family inside it, present a time problem; for them I have included a number of family and party dishes, which can be prepared in advance and finished off in a short time when required.

You will also find some recipes which are particularly good for guinea fowl or pheasant, but as both these birds are so similar to chicken in texture and size, recipes for all three birds are virtually interchangeable. Guinea fowl is a domesticated game bird which, on many hill farms, feeds on the mountainside during the day and returns to the farmer's wife for the fattening evening meal and to roost. Its beautiful black and white speckled plumage is very deceptive, as the bird inside is so much smaller! The flavour is delicately gamey, but unfortunately these birds are now being intensively produced in some areas and then processed and frozen like broiler chickens and because of this, they are not allowed to hang and they lack flavour. Pheasants are often hand-reared and sometimes frozen, but so far they are still hung and so retain their attractive gamey savour.

Today, when the cost of rearing most farm animals is continually rising, chicken production, which is a rapid process so less vulnerable to shortages than other meat, keeps poultry prices well within reach of the average family. As a result, chicken is now regularly included on many shopping lists and some of us may be tempted to fall into the trap of repeating familiar chicken dishes just because we can toss them off and no-one complains. Let us be adventurous and look abroad for fresh ideas—it is surprising how many of the exotic and exciting dishes are easy to make!

Elizabeth Pomeroy

Useful facts and figures

Oven temperature chart

	Electricity		Gas mark
	°F	°C	
Very cool	225	110	$\frac{1}{4}$
	250	130	$\frac{1}{2}$
Cool	275	140	1
	300	150	2
Moderate	325	170	3
	350	180	4
Moderately hot	375	190	5
	400	200	6
Hot	425	220	7
	450	230	8
Very hot	475	240	9

A note on metrication

In this book a basic equivalent of 25 grammes to 1 ounce has been used for solid measures and decilitres (tenths of a litre) used for liquid measures.

Each recipe has been converted individually to give a balanced result.

All cup and spoon measures in this book are level.

Notes for American users

The list below gives some American equivalents or substitutes for terms used in the book:

British	American
Cake tin	Cake pan
Cocktail stick	Wooden toothpick
Dressed weight	Ready-to-cook
Frying pan	Skillet
Gherkin	Sour pickle
Grill	Broil/Broiler
Mixer/Liquidiser	Mixer/Blender
Muslin	Cheesecloth
Patty tins	Muffin pans
Stoned	Pitted

Note: The British pint is 20 fluid ounces as opposed to the American pint which is 16 fluid ounces.

American chicken age/weight chart

Type	Age	Weight
Broiler	6–14 weeks	$\frac{3}{4}$–$2\frac{1}{2}$ lb.
Fryer	14–20 weeks	$2\frac{1}{2}$–$3\frac{1}{2}$ lb.
Roaster	5–9 months	over $3\frac{1}{2}$ lb.
Capon	about 7–10 months	over 6 lb.
Fowl or hen (female)	1 year plus	3–8 lb.

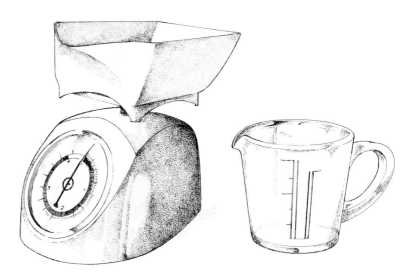

Buying birds

The marketing scene for poultry has changed remarkably during recent years. As a result of intensive production methods, the shopper is now offered what is, to some, a bewildering choice of birds of varying sizes and presumably ages; also half chickens, quarter chickens, chicken breasts and wings and legs. The labels may read 'free range' or 'farm fresh', 'pre-packed fresh' or 'frozen', so perhaps we had better start here.

'Free range' should only be applied to birds which have spent their lives pecking about out of doors in a farmyard or orchard. They, alas, are now definitely a minority group.

'Farm fresh' means that although the birds have been reared under modern methods, they come fresh, usually feathered, from the producers to the poulterer, who draws and trusses them for the customers. They have a chance to hang for a day or so, which much improves their flavour.

'Pre-packed fresh' means the birds have been dressed by the producer, then chilled and packed in transparent film without being frozen.

Frozen means they have been killed, plucked, drawn and frozen at rapid factory speed and then stored in a freezing temperature for varying periods, first by the producer and then the retailer, until bought by the customer. These birds, when whole, are best if allowed to thaw out in the refrigerator or cold larder for 24 hours before cooking. This slightly compensates for the lack of hanging previous to processing and it ensures that the bird is completely thawed out before cooking, which is absolutely essential.

Buying chart

Bird	Age	Dressed weight	Number of portions	Suitable cooking methods
Baby chickens (poussins)	4–6 weeks	1 lb. ($\frac{1}{2}$ kg.)	1–2	Spit or oven roast Split and grill or fry
Spring chickens	6–10 weeks	$1\frac{1}{2}$–2 lb. ($\frac{3}{4}$–1 kg.)	2	Spit or oven roast Split and grill or fry
Broilers	3–4 months	2–$2\frac{1}{2}$ lb. (1–$1\frac{1}{4}$ kg.)	3–4	Spit or oven roast Joint and grill or fry
Roasters	6–12 months	3–4 lb. ($1\frac{1}{2}$–$1\frac{3}{4}$ kg.)	4–5	Spit or oven roast Joint and sauté
Capons	6–12 months	5–8 lb. ($2\frac{1}{4}$–$3\frac{1}{2}$ kg.)	6–8	Oven roast
Boilers	1 year plus	$4\frac{1}{2}$–6 lb. (2–$2\frac{3}{4}$ kg.)	4–6	Simmer very slowly

Note: Any of the above birds can be pot roasted or casseroled, see recipes.

How do I choose for quality?

For roasting, grilling and frying you want a young tender bird, as plump as possible. Free range or farm fresh will have more flavour than a frozen bird. The latter are less expensive and, with the support of an interesting or exciting sauce, make a tasty dish. To test if a bird is young, bend the rear end of the breastbone—in a young tender bird this is pliable gristle, in an old bird it becomes rigid bone.

For boiling and casseroling a more mature bird may be used as it can be tenderised by long cooking at a low temperature. Boilers (not to be confused with 'broilers' which are young birds for grilling and frying) are much the cheapest. They used to be aged barnyard fowls needing half a day to cook, but nowadays, because of intensive egg production, many laying hens are killed off when only a year old and after 2½–3 hours boiling will make many delectable dishes. The younger birds have an amount of yellow fat which can be skimmed off the stock after boiling and used to add flavour to other chicken dishes like risotto.

How do I select for size?

Pre-packed and frozen chickens are sold by oven-ready weight i.e. already drawn and head and feet removed. Frozen birds are sometimes sold without giblets, so watch out if you want to make giblet stock or chicken liver stuffing. Allow about 10 oz. (275 g.) chicken per head oven-ready weight or a 2½–3-lb. (1¼–1½-kg.) roasting bird for 4 people.

Free range and farm fresh birds are also sometimes sold ready trussed, but often they are only plucked and then hung in the poulterers. They are weighed and priced before drawing and lose about 40 per cent of their weight when drawn and head and feet removed, so allow 1 lb. (½ kg.) of chicken per person, undressed weight.

If buying a roasting chicken for 6 people, a 6-lb. (2¾-kg.) capon would carve into 6 good portions. These are neutered cockerels which, being greedy and lazy, become beautifully plump and tender. (In France they also caponise hens, which are then called 'poulardes'.) These large birds, weighing from 5–8 lb. (2¼–3½ kg.), are expensive to rear and this is reflected in the price, but the flesh is of particularly high quality. For 8 people, a more economical buy would be 2 smaller birds weighing 2½–3 lb. (1¼–1½ kg.) each.

When are chicken joints a good buy?

These are sold fresh and frozen and are very useful if you want to make a dish like Chicken Kiev, in which only the breasts are used and you do not want any chicken left over. If you have time and a freezer, it is a good opportunity to make the dark meat into a casserole or other dish and freeze it for future use.

Chickens are also sold in 'quarters' and this means the bird is chopped across into four, not jointed, so the breast is halved (and cannot be stuffed) and the rib-cage and thick backbone are still attached. It is a good idea to cut these bones off, to make a little stock for gravy or a base for an interesting sauce to serve with the chicken.

Drumsticks are a convenient and economical buy for Chicken in a basket (page 18) and similar dishes.

Why must poultry be completely thawed before cooking?

Harmful bacteria tend to lurk near the bone and if the flesh around it is still frozen when the bird is put on to cook, the heat may not penetrate fully to the bone and in the semi-warmth the bacteria multiply instead of being rendered harmless by high temperature. Cut chicken portions take less time to thaw than a whole bird, but equal care must be taken to make sure they are completely thawed before grilling or frying, as they could brown outside and look appetising, while only partially cooked inside.

How do I store poultry?

Fresh poultry should be hung, before drawing, by the feet in a cool airy place and will keep like this for 2 or 3 days perfectly. Once drawn, it should be refrigerated and will keep for 2 or 3 days more. The giblets, however, should be cooked as soon as possible and refrigerated in their broth.

Frozen poultry can be stored in the freezer for several months and should be thawed out carefully before cooking, as explained above.

How do I deal with game birds?

If you live in town, game birds will be hung and dressed by the poulterer, who will advise you whether they are young enough to roast or older casserole birds. However, if a shooting friend presents you with a brace of pheasants in their beautiful plumage and you have to cope yourself, look at the legs and feet—if these are horny and the claws long, it is a sure sign of age and toughness.

Even young birds require hanging to be tender and tasty. So hang them by the neck until you can easily pull out a tuft of feathers above the tail. To pluck see below.

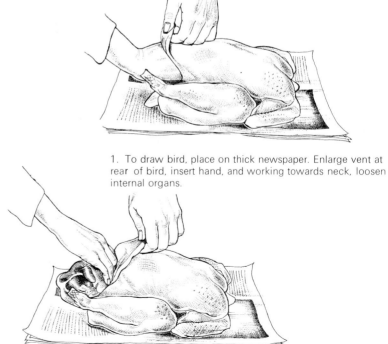

1. To draw bird, place on thick newspaper. Enlarge vent at rear of bird, insert hand, and working towards neck, loosen internal organs.

2. Draw out organs carefully all at once on to paper. Separate liver, heart and gizzard and discard intestines.

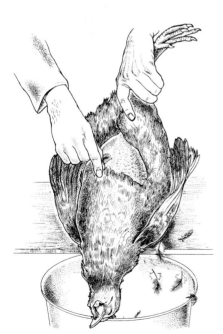

To pluck, hold bird by feet, head downwards over bin, and pluck off breast feathers, working towards head. Continue with back, wings, etc.

Bird in the oven and on the spit

Oven roasting

There are two methods of oven roasting—the fast method at high temperature (400°F, 200°C, Gas Mark 6) favoured in England, and the slow method at a lower temperature (350°F, 180°C, Gas Mark 4) preferred in U.S.A.

In France and other Continental countries, poultry is cooked in a hot oven, but stock is put in the roasting pan. This gradually evaporates, producing steam, which reduces shrinkage and keeps the bird moist. It is also basted with a buttery stock during cooking which gives it a good colour.

Covered roasting pans are used by some housewives who find them easier to clean than the oven interior, but the bird will have a similar texture to one that has been pot-roasted on top of the stove. Happily ovens are now being designed with self-cleaning linings, which is welcome progress.

Roasting in aluminium foil will prevent oven-splashing and reduce shrinkage; but except for a large bird like turkey, which is in the oven for 2–3 hours, the foil needs to be opened for the last 20 minutes despite probable splashing, if you want a crisp brown finish.

Roasting bags of transparent film allow the bird to brown during cooking and are excellent for cooking chicken joints, but a whole bird will not have quite the same texture as one that has been basted.

Cooking fats suitable for roasting poultry and game are lard, vegetable fats, unsalted or clarified butter and dripping from the same type of bird—i.e. do not mix duck, goose, turkey or game fat with chicken dripping because of the distinctive flavours. Chicken, turkey, guinea fowl and pheasant do not have a layer of fat under the skin as do duck and goose, so the breast must be protected during roasting by a covering of pork or bacon fat and well-buttered greaseproof paper, or by frequent basting if the flesh is not to become too dry.

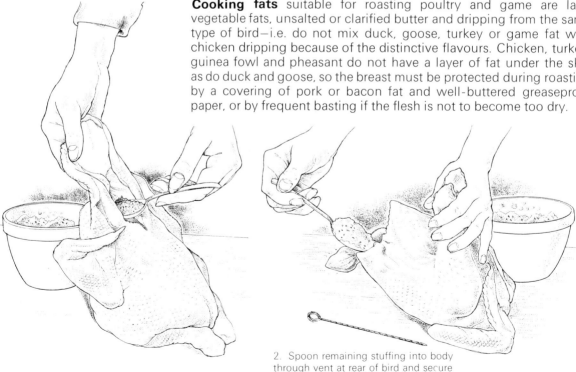

1. To stuff a chicken, draw back neck flap and pack stuffing firmly over breast. Replace flap and secure with a skewer.

2. Spoon remaining stuffing into body through vent at rear of bird and secure with a skewer.

Roast farmhouse chicken (English style)

Serves 4–5

Imperial	Metric	American
for the giblet stock:	*for the giblet stock:*	*for the giblet stock:*
giblets	giblets	giblets
1 small onion, peeled	1 small onion, peeled	1 small onion, peeled
sprig thyme and parsley	sprig thyme and parsley	sprig thyme and parsley
1 bay leaf	1 bay leaf	1 bay leaf
seasoning	seasoning	seasoning
1 roasting chicken (3½–4 lb.)	1 roasting chicken (1½–2 kg.)	1 roaster chicken (3½–4 lb.)
Rice and watercress stuffing (page 76)	Rice and watercress stuffing (page 76)	Rice and watercress stuffing (page 76)
2–3 tablespoons chicken dripping, unsalted butter or lard	2–3 tablespoons chicken dripping, unsalted butter or lard	3–4 tablespoons chicken drippings, sweet butter or lard
4 oz. streaky bacon rashers	100 g. streaky bacon rashers	¼ lb. bacon slices
watercress to garnish	watercress to garnish	watercress to garnish

Clean the giblets (page 38), put into a saucepan of cold water with the onion, herbs and seasoning, cover and simmer gently until required.

Heat the oven to 400°F, 200°C, Gas Mark 6. Make the rice and watercress stuffing, fill the breast of the chicken and truss neatly. Place the bird in a well-greased roasting pan. Remove the rind and any gristle from the bacon and cover the breast. Spread fat over the legs and cover the bird with fatted greaseproof paper or foil. Roast for 1 hour, then remove paper or foil and set the crisp bacon rashers aside and keep warm. Baste the chicken with the fat in the pan and return it to the oven for a further 15 minutes to brown the breast.

To test when the bird is ready, insert a skewer into the leg and press out a little of the juice—it will be amber coloured when cooked.

Remove the chicken to a heated carving dish and keep warm. Slowly pour the fat out of a corner of the roasting pan, leaving the residue and juices in the bottom. Add ½–¾ pint (3–4 dl., 1¼–2 cups) giblet gravy to the pan and boil briskly to reduce it and scrape the residue up from the bottom. When the gravy is a nice colour, season to taste and pour it into a warm sauce boat.

Arrange the crisped bacon rashers round the bird and garnish with fresh watercress sprigs. Serve with gravy and Bread sauce (page 61). Accompany the roast chicken with roast or jacket potatoes and cauliflower or leeks. To make larger or more portions, bake pork chipolata sausages in the oven for the last 20 minutes the chicken is cooking and arrange round the serving dish with the bacon.

1. To truss a chicken, remove feet, leaving short shanks. Secure legs firmly on either side of bird with a skewer.

2. Turn bird breast downwards and fold neck flap up over back. Insert skewer through both wings, passing it through the flap.

3. Tie legs neatly together with tail (parson's nose).

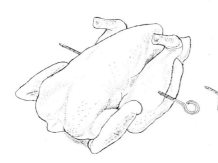

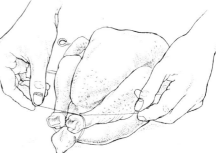

Roast tarragon chicken (French style)

Serves 4

Imperial	Metric	American
1 roasting chicken (3½ lb.)	1 roasting chicken (1½ kg.)	1 roaster chicken (3½ lb.)
2 oz. butter	50 g. butter	¼ cup butter
2 tablespoons chopped fresh tarragon leaves or 2 teaspoons crushed dried tarragon	2 tablespoons chopped fresh tarragon leaves or 2 teaspoons crushed dried tarragon	3 tablespoons chopped fresh tarragon leaves or 2 teaspoons crushed dried tarragon
1 small clove garlic	1 small clove garlic	1 small clove garlic
salt and freshly ground pepper	salt and freshly ground pepper	salt and freshly ground pepper
½ pint giblet stock (page 38)	3 dl. giblet stock (page 38)	1¼ cups giblet stock (page 38)
2 tablespoons brandy or sherry	2 tablespoons brandy or sherry	3 tablespoons brandy or sherry
4 tablespoons thick cream	4 tablespoons thick cream	⅓ cup whipping cream

Heat the oven to 400°F, 200°C, Gas Mark 6.

Truss the chicken neatly (page 9). Cream together the butter and tarragon. Skin and press the garlic and blend into the butter. Season to taste with salt and plenty of freshly ground black pepper. Spread some of the tarragon butter over the bird and put the rest inside.

Place the bird on its side on a grid in the roasting pan. Pour in the stock and bake for 20 minutes. Turn the bird on to the other side, baste and roast for another 20 minutes. Turn the chicken breast upwards and baste again. Continue roasting for another 20 minutes or until the juice runs amber-coloured when the thigh is pierced with a skewer.

Place the chicken on a heated serving dish and keep warm.

Remove the grid from the roasting pan. Pour off the fat, retaining juices. Add the brandy or sherry, boil and then stir in the cream. Season and pour into a warmed sauce boat.

Serve with potato croquettes, Courgettes au gratin (page 78) or casseroled green peas.

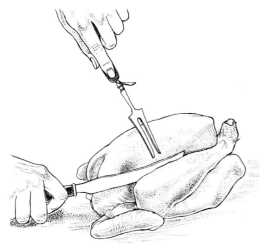

1. To carve roast chicken, secure chicken with carving fork. Insert knife between leg and body and remove drumstick and thigh in one piece

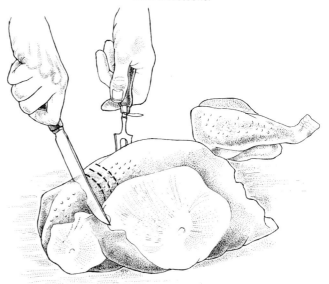

2. Insert knife behind breastbone (wishbone) and slice off front of breast. Continue slicing breast diagonally down from breastbone.

Spit roasting

This is particularly suitable for the smaller birds, chicken and game from 1–3 lb. ($\frac{1}{2}$–1$\frac{1}{2}$ kg.). The bird must be very neatly trussed (page 9) and the spit passed through it so that the weight is equally distributed or the bird will slip while revolving. As the flesh shrinks during cooking, the prongs of the fork each end of the spit may need adjusting to hold the bird secure.

The grill should be well heated and the bird basted with oil before cooking is started. Once the bird is golden brown, the heat may be slightly reduced. Frequent basting improves the texture and a sprig of thyme, rosemary or tarragon and a knob of butter inside the bird enhances the flavour. Cooking times are similar to oven roasting and gravies can be made in the same way.

Pheasant with grape stuffing

Stuff the pheasant with peeled and seeded grapes mixed with chopped tarragon leaves or a teaspoon of dried tarragon. Flavour the gravy with wine or sherry and thick double cream, or accompany with a sauce such as Hollandaise or Béarnaise blended with cream. Guinea fowl is also excellent cooked in this way.

Barbecued chicken

Illustrated in colour on page 63

Chicken is ideal for spit roasting out of doors over a charcoal brazier.

The bed of charcoal should be shallow so that it is easy to control and built up slightly behind the spit, with the heat adjustable either by regulating the draught or by raising or lowering the spit. Do not poke the charcoal because this will slow down the fire, not brighten it.

It is important not to start cooking until the flames have died down and the charcoal raked over. It should look ash grey by daylight and have a soft red glow by night.

The chicken should be well oiled and dusted liberally with paprika to give it a rosy flush. Alternatively, baste the chicken frequently with a well-seasoned marinade of soured cream (page 65) or oil and lemon juice, flavoured with finely chopped onions and herbs or with a spicy Barbecue sauce (page 62).

If cooking more than one chicken at a time, push the birds closely together, head to tail, between the spit forks.

Carve the chicken and serve with Barbecue sauce (page 62), or Tartare sauce (page 65). Accompany with baked jacket potatoes, corn on the cob or roasted sweet peppers and foil-baked peas and beans, or hot French garlic bread (page 78) and bowls of cucumber and tomato salad and tossed green salad with French dressing.

1. RIGHT. Chicken centred on spit, weight evenly distributed.

2. WRONG. Chicken unbalanced, therefore it will slip when spit revolves.

11

Bird under the grill

Cooking under a grill is the quickest and simplest method of all, but the meat must be tender and the joints small—poussins and spring chickens should be split in half and pressed flat and broilers divided into 4 or 6 joints (page 46).

(a) To keep the chicken juicy, brush with oil, melted butter, plain or savoury, or with a marinade (page 64) or a spicy sauce which contains butter, cream or oil.

(b) The grill should first be thoroughly heated and the grid greased to prevent the meat from sticking.

(c) Arrange the bird on the grid so that it is about 4 inches (10 cm.) below the flame.

(d) Grill the first side until crispy brown but not charred. Turn, brush and grill the second side. If the chicken is thick and requires further cooking, lower the heat slightly and grill for another 5–10 minutes, turning as required. If in doubt, test with a skewer in the thickest part to see if the juice is amber coloured and the chicken cooked through.

Devilled chicken legs

Serves 2

This is an excellent way of using chicken legs, whether raw or already cooked. In either case they will be more tasty if marinated in a sauce for some time prior to cooking. If the legs are from a cooked bird, make some slashes across or down them so the sauce can penetrate and prevent dryness.

Imperial	Metric	American
2 chicken legs	2 chicken legs	2 chicken legs
White or Dark devil sauce (page 64)	White or Dark devil sauce (page 64)	White or Dark devil sauce (page 64)
4–6 large flat mushrooms	4–6 large flat mushrooms	4–6 large flat mushrooms
salt and pepper	salt and pepper	salt and pepper
1½ oz. butter	40 g. butter	3 tablespoons butter
2 large tomatoes	2 large tomatoes	2 large tomatoes
sugar	sugar	sugar
4 rashers streaky bacon or 2 sausages	4 rashers streaky bacon or 2 sausages	4 bacon slices or 2 small sausages

Slash the chicken legs if pre-cooked, cover with Devil sauce and leave to marinate while preparing vegetables.

Wash or peel the mushrooms and remove the stalks. Season the dark side with salt and black pepper and dot with butter. Halve and season the tomatoes with sugar, salt and pepper.

Remove the bacon rind, roll neatly and thread on to a skewer. Heat the grill and cook the chicken legs on the first side as explained previously. Turn and coat with more sauce. Arrange on the grid the tomatoes and mushrooms, seasoned side uppermost, and the bacon rolls or sausages—turn the bacon or sausages frequently so they brown evenly. Remove the vegetables as soon as ready and, if necessary, lower the heat and cook the meat longer. Serve immediately, pouring over any sauce.

Spatchcock poussins or guinea chicks

Serves 2

Imperial	Metric	American
2 poussins or small guinea chicks	2 poussins or small guinea chicks	2 small broiler chickens or small guinea hens
3 oz. softened butter	75 g. softened butter	6 tablespoons softened butter
grated rind ½ lemon	grated rind ½ lemon	grated rind ½ lemon
1 teaspoon crushed rosemary leaves	1 teaspoon crushed rosemary leaves	1 teaspoon crushed rosemary leaves
squeeze garlic, if liked	squeeze garlic, if liked	squeeze garlic, if liked
salt and freshly ground black pepper	salt and freshly ground black pepper	salt and freshly ground black pepper
4 fl. oz. white wine	1¼ dl. white wine	½ cup white wine
4 tablespoons cream	4 tablespoons cream	⅓ cup cream
chopped fresh parsley	chopped fresh parsley	chopped fresh parsley

Split and truss the chicks spatchcock style (see below).

Cream the butter with the lemon rind, herbs and seasoning and spread generously over the fleshy side of the bird. Heat the grill, arrange the birds on the greased grid and cook the first side until golden brown. Turn, spread with more savoury butter and grill the other side.

Lower the heat and continue grilling about 5 minutes more on each side until tender. Remove each chick to a heated serving dish and keep warm.

Remove the grid from the grill pan, pour in the wine and boil to reduce, scraping up the juices from the base of the pan. Stir in the cream, adjust the seasoning and pour over the chicks. Sprinkle with freshly chopped parsley and serve at once.

Accompany with sauté potatoes and buttered spinach, peas or green beans.

1. Place chicken breast upwards and cut down centre only with poultry shears or a sharp knife, just enough to enable breastbone to be removed.
2. Remove breastbone and flatten bird with a cutlet bat or a rolling pin.
3. To truss spatchcock, fold wing pinions neatly under wings so that they lie flat. Cut off feet and push up flesh on legs to expose ends of drumsticks. Make a slit in each thigh and insert bared leg bones. Secure by inserting two skewers crosswise.

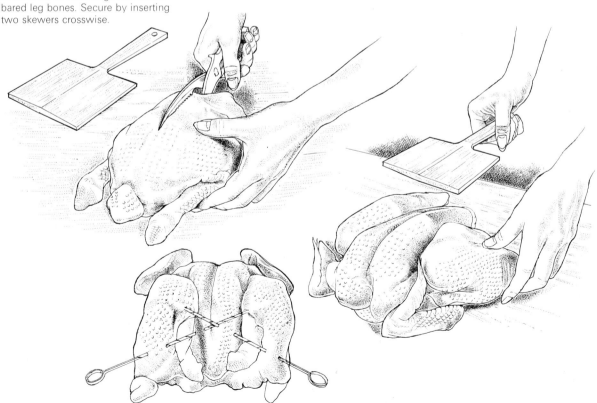

Bird in the frying pan

Shallow frying

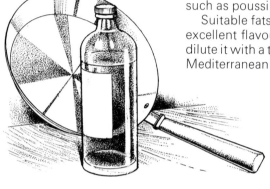

This is a quick and successful way of cooking chicken or pheasant breasts, fillets of turkey white meat and spatchcocked small birds such as poussins, young grouse and partridge.

Suitable fats are lard, clarified and unsalted butter. Butter gives an excellent flavour but as it tends to darken quickly, it is advisable to dilute it with a tasteless oil such as corn oil, or with olive oil if you like a Mediterranean flavour.

Spatchcocked spring chicken (Italian style)

Serves 2

This dish is best cooked in a shallow flame-proof casserole or a skillet i.e. a frying pan with a lid. A spring chicken or two poussins are ideal for two persons, but if cooking for four, a jointed roasting bird is easier to handle.

Imperial	Metric	American
1 spring chicken or 2 poussins	1 spring chicken or 2 poussins	1 larger or 2 small broiler chickens
seasoned flour for coating	seasoned flour for coating	seasoned flour for coating
1 oz. butter	25 g. butter	2 tablespoons butter
1 tablespoon olive oil	1 tablespoon olive oil	1 tablespoon olive oil
1 medium onion, sliced	1 medium onion, sliced	1 medium onion, sliced
2 oz. mushrooms	50 g. mushrooms	$\frac{1}{2}$ cup mushrooms
1$\frac{1}{2}$ tablespoons sherry	1$\frac{1}{2}$ tablespoons sherry	2 tablespoons sherry
1 small can Italian peeled tomatoes	1 small can Italian peeled tomatoes	1 small can Italian peeled tomatoes
pinch fresh basil or marjoram	pinch fresh basil or marjoram	pinch fresh basil or marjoram
salt and freshly ground black pepper	salt and freshly ground black pepper	salt and freshly ground black pepper
lemon juice to taste	lemon juice to taste	lemon juice to taste

Truss the chicken spatchcock style (page 13) and coat with seasoned flour, patting off surplus.

Heat the butter and oil and fry the chicken until nicely browned, turning once. Remove from the pan and fry the onion gently until softened. Wash the mushrooms, halve if large, add to the pan and continue frying until the onion starts to colour. Pour in the sherry and boil up. Stir in the tomatoes and herbs, season and add lemon juice to taste. Add the chicken, cover and simmer gently for 20 minutes, or until tender.

Serve with a bowl of buttered tagliatelli or other pasta and Spinach croquettes (page 78).

Chicken or pheasant breasts with apricots and brandy

Serves 2

This is a delightful dish for a *diner à deux*. The breasts from a 3½-lb. (1½-kg.) bird will weigh about 4 oz. (100 g.) each and one per portion will be sufficient. If using smaller birds, two may be required. The legs from the game birds are handy for pâtés and pies.

Imperial	Metric	American
2 oz. dried apricots	50 g. dried apricots	⅓ cup dried apricots
2–4 chicken or pheasant breasts	2–4 chicken or pheasant breasts	2–4 chicken or pheasant breasts
seasoned flour for coating	seasoned flour for coating	seasoned flour for coating
1 oz. unsalted butter	25 g. unsalted butter	2 tablespoons sweet butter
1 tablespoon vegetable oil	1 tablespoon vegetable oil	1 tablespoon vegetable oil
1 tablespoon brandy	1 tablespoon brandy	1 tablespoon brandy
2–3 tablespoons soured cream	2–3 tablespoons soured cream	3–4 tablespoons sour cream
lemon juice, salt and pepper to taste	lemon juice, salt and pepper to taste	lemon juice, salt and pepper to taste
toasted flaked almonds or chopped walnuts for garnish	toasted flaked almonds or chopped walnuts for garnish	toasted flaked almonds or chopped walnuts for garnish

The apricots can be plumped by soaking overnight, or put into a saucepan with cold water to cover, gradually heated and simmered gently for 10 minutes until partially cooked—they are best slightly undercooked or they will go mushy in the sauce.

Fillet the chicken breasts (see below) carefully off the bone, removing the pinions. Put between sheets of greaseproof paper and beat out flat so they resemble veal escalopes. Coat in seasoned flour, rubbing it in well. Heat the butter and oil in a frying pan and fry the breasts briskly until golden brown, turning once. Lower the heat. Drain the apricots, setting the liquid aside, and add to the pan.

Warm the brandy in a soup ladle or tiny saucepan, set it alight and pour it flaming over the chicken. Shake the pan until the flames die down. Mix ¼ pint (1½ dl., ⅔ cup) of the apricot liquor into the cream and stir this into the pan. Season to taste and simmer for 5 minutes or until the chicken is tender. Add extra apricot liquor if there is not quite enough sauce.

Serve at once in a border of fluffy boiled rice or buttered noodles. Sprinkle the chicken with toasted flaked almonds or chopped walnuts.

Accompany with Courgettes au gratin (page 78) or buttered French beans.

Variations:
Double cream sharpened with lemon juice may be used instead of soured cream.
Whisky may be used in place of brandy.

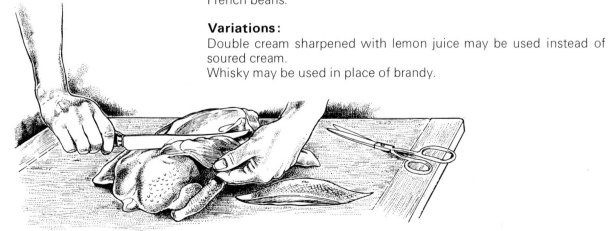

Filleting chicken breasts

Deep frying

Chicken quarters or joints are easier to cook successfully in deep fat, rather than in a shallow frying pan. The chicken pieces should always be coated in egg and breadcrumbs or batter to prevent the juices from seeping out. The heat of the fat must be carefully controlled so that the outside of the joints are crisp, whilst the chicken is cooked right through to the centre. Follow the instructions for deep frying below and on page 18.

Maryland chicken

Serves 4

This traditional dish from the Southern States of America is a firm favourite on both sides of the Atlantic. A small, tender chicken should be chosen, as long frying tends to darken the golden coating. The electric frying pan is an excellent ally, because the temperature is so easily controlled, but any deep, thick frying pan will do.

Imperial	Metric	American
1 roasting chicken (2–2½ lb.)	1 roasting chicken (1–1¼ kg.)	1 broiler–fryer chicken (2–2½ lb.)
2 oz. seasoned flour	50 g. seasoned flour	½ cup seasoned flour
1 egg, beaten	1 egg, beaten	1 egg, beaten
1 tablespoon water	1 tablespoon water	1 tablespoon water
fresh white breadcrumbs	fresh white breadcrumbs	fresh white bread crumbs
deep fat for frying	deep fat for frying	deep fat for frying
¼ pint chicken stock	1½ dl. chicken stock	⅔ cup chicken stock
¼ pint cream	1½ dl. cream	⅔ cup cream
1 oz. butter	25 g. butter	2 tablespoons butter
for garnish:	*for garnish:*	*for garnish:*
corn fritters (page 78)	corn fritters (page 78)	corn fritters (page 78)
4 crisp bacon rashers	4 crisp bacon rashers	4 crisp bacon slices
4 small fried bananas	4 small fried bananas	4 small fried bananas
lemon wedges	lemon wedges	lemon wedges

Joint and skin chicken (pages 45 and 46). Divide legs into 2 joints and separate the wings from the breasts. Flour the joints, patting off any loose grains. Beat the egg and water together and brush over each joint. Place it on a bed of crumbs, cover with more crumbs and press well in. Shake off any surplus and set aside for the coating to harden for 1 hour or longer.

Heat about 1 inch (2½ cm.) of fat in a large, thick frying pan to 380°F, 190°C, (page 18). Give each joint a final shake and fry until golden underneath, pressing the wings flat if they curl out of the fat. Turn the joints and fry on the other side until golden. Lower the heat slightly and continue frying for about 10 minutes each side, a total of 35–40 minutes.

Cover during cooking with a ventilated lid or, if the lid has no vent, tilt it so that the steam can escape. Drain the cooked chicken on soft, absorbent paper and keep warm.

Fry the corn fritters in the hot fat, drain and keep warm. Carefully pour off the fat, leaving the juices in the pan. Stir in a tablespoon of seasoned flour and fry, stirring for a few minutes. Blend in the stock and cream, simmer gently for 3 minutes and pour into a warm sauce boat. Meanwhile in another pan, fry the bacon crisp, remove and add the butter. Peel and halve the bananas lengthwise and fry briskly.

Arrange the chicken on a warm serving dish and garnish with the fritters, bacon, bananas and lemon. Serve with the sauce.

Chicken Kiev

Serves 4

This recipe uses only the breasts and wings of each bird; provision should be made for using up the rest in casseroles, pies or rice dishes.

Chicken Kiev requires careful preparation, but it can be kept overnight in the refrigerator before frying or deep frozen for future use.

Imperial	Metric	American
2 roasting chickens (2½–3 lb.)	2 roasting chickens (1–1½ kg.)	2 broiler–fryer chickens (2½–3 lb.)
4 oz. softened unsalted butter	100 g. softened unsalted butter	½ cup softened sweet butter
grated rind and juice 1 lemon	grated rind and juice 1 lemon	grated rind and juice 1 lemon
1½ tablespoons chopped fresh parsley	1½ tablespoons chopped fresh parsley	2 tablespoons chopped fresh parsley
1 teaspoon tarragon or rosemary	1 teaspoon tarragon or rosemary	1 teaspoon tarragon or rosemary
pinch ground nutmeg or mace	pinch ground nutmeg or mace	pinch ground nutmeg or mace
salt and freshly ground black pepper	salt and freshly ground black pepper	salt and freshly ground black pepper
seasoned flour for coating	seasoned flour for coating	seasoned flour for coating
1 egg	1 egg	1 egg
fresh breadcrumbs for coating	fresh breadcrumbs for coating	fresh bread crumbs for coating
deep fat for frying	deep fat for frying	deep fat for frying

Carefully fillet the 2 sides of the breast of each chicken with the wing bone attached and beat flat (see this page).

Cream together the butter, lemon rind and herbs and flavour to taste with lemon juice, spice and seasoning. Shape into a rectangle and chill until hard. Cut into 4 pieces, lay one on each chicken breast, fold and roll up neatly, pressing well together. Roll in seasoned flour and pat off surplus. Coat with beaten egg and crumbs, see Chicken in a basket (page 18). Coat a second time for a perfect finish. Chill well before frying—leave overnight if preferred.

Heat the deep fat to 375°–380°F, 190°–195°C, put the chicken into the greased frying basket and cook until golden brown (page 18). Drain on soft paper, put a cutlet frill on the wing bone and serve immediately. Garnish with lemon wedges and parsley.

Serve with French fried or soufflé potatoes and a tossed green salad.

Note: It may be advisable to warn guests that the melted butter will spurt out unless care is taken when cutting into the chicken.

1. Beat chicken breast flat with a cutlet bat or rolling pin.

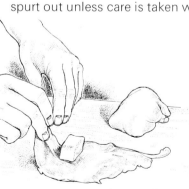
2. Place a portion of savoury butter on the centre of breast and roll up neatly, enclosing butter completely.

3. Coat twice with beaten egg and crumbs. Chill well before frying

Chicken in a basket

Illustrated in colour opposite
Serves 4–6

This is the simplest way to fry chicken and is an ideal dish to serve hot at a fork-and-finger party in the garden or cold at a picnic.

For large parties it is more economical to buy trays of drumsticks and/or chicken breasts instead of jointing whole chickens. The drumsticks are most convenient to hold in the fingers.

Imperial	Metric	American
6 chicken drumsticks	6 chicken drumsticks	6 chicken drumsticks
seasoned flour for coating	seasoned flour for coating	seasoned flour for coating
1 egg, beaten	1 egg, beaten	1 egg, beaten
4 teaspoons Dijon mustard	4 teaspoons Dijon mustard	4 teaspoons Dijon mustard
about 6 oz. fresh breadcrumbs	about 175 g. fresh breadcrumbs	about 3 cups fresh bread crumbs
4 tablespoons grated cheese	4 tablespoons grated cheese	$\frac{1}{3}$ cup grated cheese
deep fat for frying	deep fat for frying	deep fat for frying
watercress for garnish	watercress for garnish	watercress for garnish

Wipe and dry the chicken, thaw out thoroughly if frozen. Toss in seasoned flour, patting off surplus. Beat the egg and gradually blend into the mustard.

Mix together the breadcrumbs and grated cheese and make a bed of this on a piece of greaseproof paper. Take the joints, one at a time, and brush carefully all over with egg and mustard. Then place on the bed of crumbs and cheese and, by tipping the paper, roll the joint over in the crumbs until completely coated. Press the crumbs in firmly. Shake off any surplus and leave the coating to harden before deep frying (see below).

After frying, drain on soft paper. Cover the protruding ends of the bones with cutlet frills, if liked. Arrange in a basket lined with a napkin, and garnish with watercress or parsley sprigs.

To deep fry, fill pan two-thirds full with oil or cooking fat and heat, with basket, to 375°F. (190°C.), or until a cube of bread becomes golden brown and floats in just under 1 minute. Lift out basket and place chicken joints in it. Lower carefully into hot fat and fry until golden, about 8–10 minutes.

Serving suggestions:
(a) Serve hot with tomato or Barbecue sauce (page 62). Accompany with jacket potatoes stuffed with cottage cheese and chopped chives or hot potato and crispy bacon salad, or French garlic bread (page 78).
(b) Serve cold with Tartare or Gribiche sauce (page 65). Accompany with salads, which can be dressed in advance and easily eaten with a fork—tomato, cucumber, green peppers and chopped spring onions with French dressing. Chicory, apple, celery and beetroot with sour cream dressing and new potato salad.

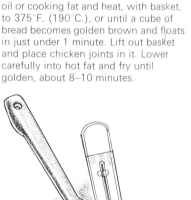

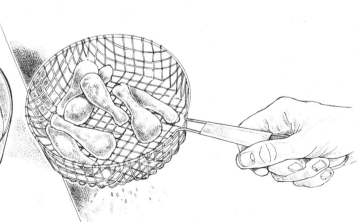

Bird in pies and pastries

Crispy golden pastry, as well as contributing to variety in menus, is a marvellous 'stretcher' of poultry or game.

A pheasant past roasting can be transformed into an impressive game pie, and as little as 4 oz. (100 g.) cooked chicken meat will make a tasty filling for Kromeskies, or 6 oz. (175 g.) for Alsatian chicken and cheese tart (pages 24 and 73).

Chicken or pheasant en croûte

Serves 4

The top chefs' style for this dish is a whole bird, boned and filled with a rich stuffing; roasted French style and then wrapped in puff pastry, elaborately decorated and baked. The following recipe, using chicken or pheasant joints, is an easy but delicious version for the home cook to make.

Imperial	Metric	American
4 joints (from a young bird)	4 joints (from a young bird)	4 pieces (from a broiler chicken)
1 (13 oz.) packet frozen puff pastry	1 (368 g.) packet frozen puff pastry	1 (13 oz.) package frozen puff paste
5 tablespoons cranberry and orange relish or apricot or similar chutney	5 tablespoons cranberry and orange relish or apricot or similar chutney	6 tablespoons cranberry and orange relish or apricot or similar chutney
1 egg, beaten	1 egg, beaten	1 egg, beaten
1 tablespoon water	1 tablespoon water	1 tablespoon water

The joints can be breasts, thighs or drumsticks, as available. If the croûtes are to be eaten hot, remove the bones neatly and press the flesh back together. If they are to be eaten cold at a picnic, choose chicken drumsticks and leave the end of the bone protruding from the pastry. When cooked, it can be covered with a frill and held in the fingers.

Roll the pastry out very thinly. Space the joints out on it as shown and cut round. Lift up each joint, one at a time, spread with relish on both sides and place it back on the pastry.

Beat the egg and water together and brush round the edge. Place the pastry over the joint and press the edges firmly together. Knock up with the back of a knife. Brush all over with beaten egg. Decorate with little leaves, cut from the pastry trimmings and glazed with egg. Make 2 or 3 slits for the steam to escape during baking.

Bake in preheated oven (425°F, 220°C, Gas Mark 7) for 15 minutes until well risen and golden. Reduce the heat (375°F, 190°C, Gas Mark 5) and continue baking for 15–20 minutes, until the joints are thoroughly cooked. Serve hot or cold with tossed salad.

Variation:
For a richer dish, mix 2 oz. (50 g.) finely chopped mushrooms with 2 oz. (50 g.) liver pâté and spread this on the chicken joints, instead of the relish or chutney.

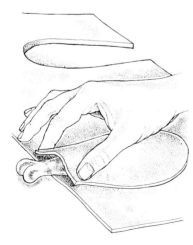

Welsh leek and chicken pie

Illustrated in colour on page 23
Serves 6

This pie has a particularly tasty filling of chicken mixed with a creamy leek and bacon sauce. A small boiling fowl will make a large family-sized pie, and the same recipe with reduced quantities, using surplus cooked chicken, can be used as a flavoursome filling for Vols-au-vent (page 29), Piroshki (page 25) and Kromeskies (page 73).

Imperial	Metric	American
1 small boiled boiling fowl (page 42)	1 small boiled boiling fowl (page 42)	1 small boiled stewing chicken (page 42)
8 oz. leeks	225 g. leeks	$\frac{1}{2}$ lb. leeks
4 oz. bacon rashers or ham trimmings	100 g. bacon rashers or ham trimmings	$\frac{1}{4}$ lb. bacon slices or ham trimmings
1 oz. butter	25 g. butter	2 tablespoons butter
1½ tablespoons flour	1½ tablespoons flour	2 tablespoons flour
$\frac{3}{4}$ pint chicken stock	scant $\frac{1}{2}$ litre chicken stock	2 cups chicken stock
$\frac{1}{4}$ pint single cream	1½ dl. single cream	$\frac{2}{3}$ cup coffee cream
salt, pepper and lemon juice to taste	salt, pepper and lemon juice to taste	salt, pepper and lemon juice to taste
1 (13 oz.) packet frozen puff pastry	1 (368 g.) packet frozen puff pastry	1 (13 oz.) package frozen puff paste
1 beaten egg for glazing	1 beaten egg for glazing	1 beaten egg for glazing

Skin the chicken, remove the flesh from the bones and cut into chunks.

Clean the leeks, remove most of the green and cut into $\frac{1}{2}$-inch (1-cm.) slices. Remove the rind and gristle from the bacon and chop across into strips. Heat slowly in a thick saucepan until the fat runs and the bacon begins to crisp. Add the butter and, when melted, the leeks. Cover and cook gently, without colouring, until softened. Stir frequently. Remove the pan from the heat and blend in the flour and then two-thirds of the chicken stock. Simmer and cook for 5 minutes, stirring well. Blend the remaining stock into the cream. Remove the leek sauce from the heat and stir in the cream mixture. Season well and sharpen with lemon juice. Mix in the chicken pieces.

Put a pie funnel in the centre of a large pie dish and surround with the chicken filling.

Roll out the pastry, cover, decorate and glaze the pie. Bake in a preheated oven, 450°F, 230°C, Gas Mark 8, for 10–15 minutes until well risen. Lower heat to 400°F, 200°C, Gas Mark 6 and continue cooking for another 20 minutes or until crisp and golden.

To decorate a pie crust, cut pastry strips about 1½ inches (4 cm.) wide.
Cut them quarter of the way across to form a fringe. Roll up round skewer with point protruding 1 inch (2½ cm.) beyond uncut edge. Insert skewer in top of pie funnel and press base of pastry flower on to the pie. Remove skewer and with it open pastry petals.

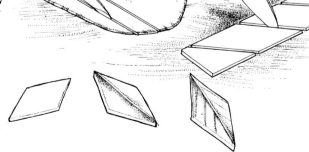

To make leaves, cut another strip 1½ inches (4 cm.) wide and cut diagonally across into diamond-shaped leaves. Mark veins with the back of knife.

Chicken and ham pie à la Russe

Illustrated in colour opposite
Serves 4–6

This attractive dish is delightfully quick to make if frozen pastry is used. The ingredients for the filling can be varied to use up cooked chicken meat and ham as available. The cheese melts during baking and makes the filling succulent as well as savoury.

Imperial	Metric	American
4–5 oz. cooked chicken, chopped	100–150 g. cooked chicken, chopped	$\frac{1}{2}$–$\frac{2}{3}$ cup chopped cooked chicken
2 oz. cooked ham, cubed	50 g. cooked ham, cubed	$\frac{1}{3}$ cup cubed cooked ham
5 oz. Cheddar cheese, cubed	150 g. Cheddar cheese, cubed	generous $\frac{3}{4}$ cup cubed Cheddar cheese
2 oz. mushrooms, chopped	50 g. mushrooms, chopped	$\frac{1}{2}$ cup chopped mushrooms
1 tablespoon chopped parsley	1 tablespoon chopped parsley	1 tablespoon chopped parsley
salt and ground black pepper	salt and ground black pepper	salt and ground black pepper
1 beaten egg to bind	1 beaten egg to bind	1 beaten egg to bind
8 oz. frozen puff pastry	225 g. frozen puff pastry	$\frac{1}{2}$ lb. frozen puff paste
1 beaten egg for glazing	1 beaten egg for glazing	1 beaten egg for glazing

Mix together the chicken, ham, cheese, mushrooms and parsley. Season to taste. Stir 1 beaten egg into the mixture. Roll the pastry thinly into a rectangle 15 × 10 inches (39 × 26 cm.). Cut out a square 10 × 10 inches (26 × 26 cm.) (below). Place on a baking tray. Pile the filling in the centre. Fold the corners of the square to the centre and seal with beaten egg. Brush all over the pie evenly with egg. Use remaining pastry to make decorations and tassel (page 21), glaze with egg and arrange on pie. Open the outer corners of the envelope slightly to allow steam to escape during cooking.

Bake in a preheated oven (425°F, 220°C, Gas Mark 7) for 25 minutes until well risen and golden brown. Serve hot, garnished with tomato quarters and fresh watercress.

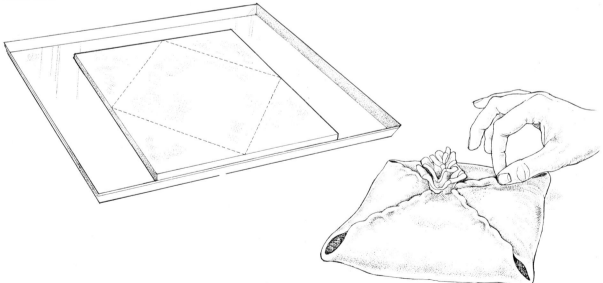

1. Place pastry square on a baking sheet. Place filling in dotted area.

2. Flute sealed edges of pie and decorate with pastry rose or cut out pastry shapes.

Chicken and ham pie à la Russe (see recipe opposite), Welsh leek and chicken pie (page 21), Alsatian chicken and cheese tart (page 24) *and* Chicken or game piroshki (page 25)

Alsatian chicken and cheese tart

Illustrated in colour on page 23
Serves 4–6

This tart served hot makes an appetising main course for lunch or supper. It is good picnic fare when served cold.

Imperial	Metric	American
6 oz. shortcrust pastry (using 6 oz. flour etc.) (page 25)	175 g. shortcrust pastry (using 175 g. flour etc.) (page 25)	$\frac{1}{3}$ lb. shortcrust paste (using $1\frac{1}{2}$ cups flour etc.) (page 25)
1 oz. butter	25 g. butter	2 tablespoons butter
2 rashers streaky bacon, chopped	2 rashers streaky bacon, chopped	2 bacon slices, chopped
1 small onion, chopped	1 small onion, chopped	1 small onion, chopped
8 fl. oz. cream	$2\frac{1}{2}$ dl. cream	1 cup cream
2 oz. cheese, grated	50 g. cheese, grated	$\frac{1}{2}$ cup grated cheese
6 oz. cooked chicken meat	175 g. cooked chicken meat	$\frac{1}{3}$ lb. cooked chicken meat
1 egg, beaten	1 egg, beaten	1 egg, beaten
paprika, salt and black pepper	paprika, salt and black pepper	paprika, salt and black pepper

Roll out the pastry thinly. Damp the lip of an 8-inch (20-cm.) shallow pie plate and press on $\frac{1}{2}$-inch (1-cm.) wide strips of pastry. Brush with water. Roll the remaining pastry round the rolling pin and unroll across the pie plate. Ease the pastry lining into the dish and press firmly round the edge to prevent shrinkage in the oven. Trim neatly and knock up the edges with the back of the knife. Using a small fluted cutter, cut pastry circles out of the trimmings. Dampen the pastry on the lip of the dish and press on the circles, marking the centre of each one with a skewer. Prick over the base of the pie.

Heat the butter in a small pan and fry the bacon and onion slowly until just colouring. Add the cream and heat until nearly boiling. Remove from the heat and stir in the cheese. When melted add the chicken. Stir in the beaten egg and season well with paprika, salt and freshly ground pepper.

Pour the mixture into the pie and bake in a preheated oven (375°F, 190°C, Gas Mark 5) for 20 minutes or until set and nicely coloured.

Serve hot or cold with asparagus spears or a mixed salad tossed in French dressing.

1 Press a $\frac{1}{2}$-inch (1-cm.) wide strip of pastry round lip of pie plate.

2. Ease pastry lining into dish and press firmly round edges

3. Knock up edge with back of a knife.

4. Press pastry decorations round dampened rim.

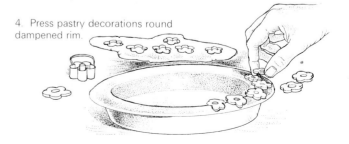

Chicken or game piroshki

Illustrated in colour on page 23
Makes 8 piroshki

These little Polish pasties are ideal for a fireside supper or hot buffet dish. They can be made with shortcrust or flaky pastry and any available mixture of chicken, game, pork or ham.

Imperial	Metric	American
2 large shallots	2 large shallots	2 large shallots
2 oz. mushrooms, chopped	50 g. mushrooms, chopped	½ cup chopped mushrooms
2 oz. belly pork or ham, diced	50 g. belly pork or ham, diced	⅓ cup diced pork or cooked ham
1 oz. butter	25 g. butter	2 tablespoons butter
4 oz. cooked chicken or game, chopped	100 g. cooked chicken or game, chopped	½ cup chopped cooked chicken or game
1 teaspoon dried savory or rosemary	1 teaspoon dried savory or rosemary	1 teaspoon dried savory or rosemary
1 tablespoon chopped fresh parsley	1 tablespoon chopped fresh parsley	1 tablespoon chopped fresh parsley
salt and freshly ground black pepper	salt and freshly ground black pepper	salt and freshly ground black pepper
3–4 tablespoons soured cream	3–4 tablespoons soured cream	4–5 tablespoons sour cream
8 oz. shortcrust or flaky pastry (using 8 oz. flour etc.)	225 g. shortcrust or flaky pastry (using 225 g. flour etc.)	½ lb. shortcrust pastry or puff paste (using 2 cups all-purpose flour etc.)
beaten egg for glazing	beaten egg for glazing	beaten egg for glazing

Fry the finely sliced shallots, mushrooms and pork slowly in the butter until slightly crisp. Mix in the chicken or game and herbs and cook gently until well buttered. Season well, stir in the soured cream (or double cream sharpened with lemon juice) and leave to cool

Roll out the pastry thinly. Cut out 8 circles and line Yorkshire pudding or deep patty tins. Spoon in the filling. Cut 8 smaller circles out of the remaining pastry. Damp the pastry edges and press the lids in place, pinching the edges firmly together. Crimp with a fork. Brush the tops with beaten egg and cut little slits in the centre for the steam to escape. Bake in a preheated oven (425°F, 220°C, Gas Mark 7) until crisp and golden.

Shortcrust pastry

Imperial	Metric	American
8 oz. flour	225 g. flour	2 cups all-purpose flour
pinch salt	pinch salt	pinch salt
4 oz. butter, margarine or lard	125 g. butter, margarine or lard	½ cup butter, margarine or lard

Sift the flour and salt into a mixing bowl. Cut up the fat and, with the tips of the fingers, rub it into the flour until the mixture resembles breadcrumbs. Hold the hands well above the bowl to aerate the mixture and keep it cool. Shake the bowl to bring the larger crumbs to the surface for rubbing in. Do not over-rub or fat will become oily and pastry heavy. Add cold water, a tablespoon at a time, and stir it in with a palette knife until the mixture binds into a soft, but not sticky, dough. Too much water makes the pastry heavy, too little will make it crumbly. Gather it together with one hand, it should leave the sides of the bowl clean. Turn on to a floured board and knead lightly until cracks disappear. Leave in a cool place until required.

Raised game or chicken pie

Illustrated in colour opposite
Serves 4–6

Cold game pie can be made with any combination of furred or feathered game and poultry. Older game birds may be used but must be well hung before cooking. The knuckle of veal provides extra meat as well as providing jelly in the stock.

Imperial	Metric	American
1½ oz. butter	40 g. butter	3 tablespoons butter
1 pheasant or chicken	1 pheasant or chicken	1 pheasant or chicken
8 oz. pickled belly pork	225 g. pickled belly pork	½ lb. salt pork
1 knuckle veal, in 2–3 pieces	1 knuckle veal, in 2–3 pieces	1 veal shank, in 2–3 pieces
1 onion, sliced	1 onion, sliced	1 onion, sliced
1–2 sticks celery, chopped	1–2 sticks celery, chopped	1–2 stalks celery, chopped
2–3 carrots, scraped	2–3 carrots, scraped	2–3 carrots, cleaned
bouquet garni	bouquet garni	bouquet garni
4 fl. oz. red wine	1¼ dl. red wine	½ cup red wine
seasoning	seasoning	seasoning
1 quantity hot water crust pastry (page 29)	1 quantity hot water crust pastry (page 29)	1 quantity hot water crust pastry (page 29)
egg for glazing	egg for glazing	egg for glazing

Heat the butter in a flameproof casserole and brown the bird all over or roast in a quick oven (425°F, 220°C, Gas Mark 7) for 15 minutes. Lift out of casserole, remove the breasts and set aside. Put the pork, cut in chunks, veal and onion in the hot butter and fry gently until just coloured. Break up and add the carcass and cleaned giblets, the celery, carrots, herbs and wine. Cover with cold water, season well and bring to the boil. Cover and simmer gently for 2 hours. (For a chicken pie, remove thighs when tender.) Strain stock and leave to cool into a jelly. Skim off the fat. Remove the flesh from the carcass and veal knuckle, and mince or chop finely. Discard the bones, vegetables and herbs but retain the pork chunks. Cut the breast of the bird (and chicken thighs) into neat pieces. Line the pie mould, or 6-inch (15-cm.) cake tin with a loose base, with hot water crust pastry. Season the minced meat to taste and spread over the base of the pie. Fill up with well mixed game or chicken and pork meat, moisten with a very little stock.

Cover, decorate (page 21) and glaze with beaten egg, making slits in the top. Bake in a preheated oven (400°F, 200°C, Gas Mark 6) for 30 minutes or until golden brown and set. Open mould and remove sides. If using a cake tin, stand it on an inverted jam jar and carefully push down the sides of the tin, leaving the mould on the base. Brush the sides of the pie with beaten egg, cover the top with greaseproof paper, return to the oven and bake for a further 20–30 minutes until the sides are golden brown.

Meanwhile check that the stock has set into jelly, if not boil until reduced, correct seasoning and cool.

Remove the pie from the oven and, using a little funnel, carefully pour the cool liquid jelly through the slits into the pie, or through the hole under the pastry rose or tassel, giving it time to trickle between the meat chunks and fill the crevices.

Serve the pie, when cold, with cranberry relish or apricot chutney. Accompany with potato and other dressed salads in season.

Raised game or chicken pie (see recipe opposite) *and* Vols-au-vent (page 29)

To make a raised pie (see recipe page 26)

1. Shape the hot water crust into a fat sausage. Cut off one third and reserve in a polythene bag to keep warm.

2. Roll out remaining dough on a floured board into an oval about ½ inch (1 cm.) thick.

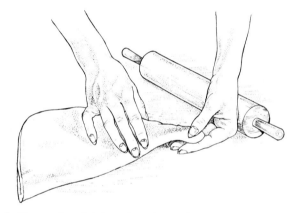

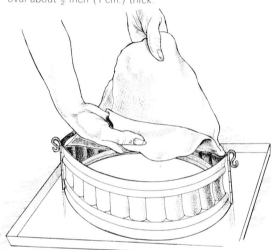

3. Flour surface lightly and evenly and fold oval in half to make a semi-circle. Pull ends of semi-circle away from you to form a crescent shape. With a floured rolling pin, roll lightly away from you until dough is ½ inch (1 cm.) thick. Do not press heavily or dough will stick together.

4. Now gently open out folded pastry and slip it into greased pie mould, placed on a baking sheet. Press dough evenly over base, well into corners and up sides of mould. Put in filling.

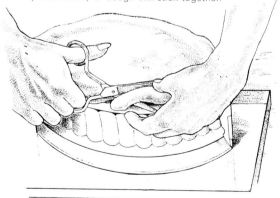

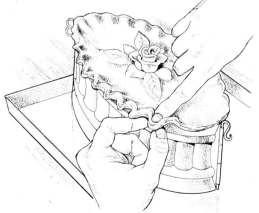

5. Roll out remaining dough ¼ inch (½ cm.) thick to make a lid. Brush rim of dough lining mould with water, place lid in position and press edges firmly together. Trim edges with scissors and mark evenly with back of a knife to make neat edging.

6. Crimp edge with fingers and use dough trimmings to decorate the top (page 21).

Hot water crust pastry

Imperial	Metric	American
10 oz. flour	275 g. flour	2½ cups all-purpose flour
¼ teaspoon salt	¼ teaspoon salt	¼ teaspoon salt
3 oz. lard or cooking fat	75 g. lard or cooking fat	6 tablespoons lard or shortening
¼ pint water	1½ dl. water	⅔ cup water

Sift the flour and salt into a warm mixing bowl. Put the fat and water into a small saucepan over a low heat. When the fat has dissolved, bring the liquid to the boil. Pour immediately into the flour, stirring with a wooden spoon and beat into a ball. Knead on a floured board until a smooth ball. Put in a polythene bag, wrap in a warm tea towel and keep warm until required.

Hot vol-au-vents

Illustrated in colour on page 27

These are always popular and can be made quite tiny for cocktail savouries or full size for a main course.

Make or buy vol-au-vent cases. Heat the cases and, when ready to serve, fill with hot Cheesy chicken à la King (page 72) or chopped cooked chicken in Blanquette or Cheese béchamel sauce (pages 60 and 61). If they are filled before heating, the pastry cases will not be so crisp.

Cold vol-au-vents

Make or buy extra light puff pastry cases if they are to be eaten cold, as they will not be crisped by reheating. Fill with chopped chicken and cucumber mixed with Tunny fish mayonnaise (page 65), or combined with diced cooked tongue or lean ham and mixed with Gribiche sauce (page 65).

To make vol-au-vent cases, cut out circles of pastry with a plain cutter. Cut out centres of half the pastry circles to make rings. Brush one side of each ring with water and press firmly on to a base.

Cold bird

Poultry and game can be made into a wide variety of attractive cold dishes. It can be boiled, or oven or spit-roasted and, when cold, served with a rich sauce to counterbalance any dryness. Smaller quantities can be chopped to make a salad or mousse.

Chicken salamagundy

Illustrated in colour opposite
Serves 6–8

Salamagundy was considered 'a fine middle dish' for a fashionable table in 18th-century England and the modern version makes a splendid centre piece for a buffet table to which the guests can help themselves.

Imperial	Metric	American
1 cooked chicken (3½–4 lb.)	1 cooked chicken (1½–2 kg.)	1 cooked chicken (3½–4 lb.)
1 bunch spring onions	1 bunch spring onions	1 bunch scallions
¼ pint thick mayonnaise (page 65)	1½ dl. thick mayonnaise (page 65)	⅔ cup thick mayonnaise (page 65)
1 tablespoon chopped fresh parsley	1 tablespoon chopped fresh parsley	1 tablespoon chopped fresh parsley
¼ pint double cream	1½ dl. double cream	⅔ cup whipping cream
1 lemon	1 lemon	1 lemon
salt and pepper	salt and pepper	salt and pepper
2 hard-boiled eggs	2 hard-boiled eggs	2 hard-cooked eggs
½ cucumber, sliced	½ cucumber, sliced	½ cucumber, sliced
1 bunch watercress	1 bunch watercress	1 bunch watercress
1 lettuce	1 lettuce	1 head lettuce
2 oz. mushrooms	50 g. mushrooms	½ cup mushrooms
1 bunch radishes	1 bunch radishes	1 bunch radishes
¼ pint French dressing	1½ dl. French dressing	⅔ cup French dressing

Skin the chicken. Slice the chicken breast into fingers and set aside. Remove the flesh from the legs and the rest of the carcass and chop into small pieces. Clean the spring onions leaving 2–3 inches (5–7½ cm.) of green. Chop them finely and add to the mayonnaise, which must be very thick. Stir in the parsley. Whip the cream until thick and fold in the mayonnaise.

Peel and chop the lemon, removing pith and skin and mix it with the chopped chicken. Stir in sufficient cream and mayonnaise mixture to bind. Season to taste with salt and pepper.

Separate the yolks and whites of the eggs. Sieve the yolks to make mimosa and chop the whites with a stainless steel knife. Pile the chicken mayonnaise mixture into the centre of a large round dish and decorate the top of the mound with circles of mimosa egg, chopped white and chopped parsley.

Surround with circles of sliced cucumber, washed watercress sprigs and arrange mushroom slices and prepared lettuce leaves round the outside of the dish. Arrange the chicken fingers on the watercress. Wash and trim the radishes and put one between each chicken finger. Sprinkle the chicken with mimosa egg. Just before serving, sprinkle the green salad with French dressing.

Chicken salamagundy (see recipe opposite)
and Chicken and ham mousse (page 34)

Cold galantine of chicken

Serves 6–8

This is an excellent dish for a cold buffet or luncheon party, as the boned and stuffed bird presents no carving problems and looks very attractive when decorated and glazed with chaudfroid sauce or aspic jelly. Boning the chicken and cooling the sauce and jelly to the right consistency can be tricky, but very rewarding for the fairly experienced and adventurous cook.

Imperial	Metric	American
1 boiling fowl	1 boiling fowl	1 stewing chicken
1 knuckle veal	1 knuckle veal	1 veal shank
vegetables, herbs and seasoning for chicken stock (page 38)	vegetables, herbs and seasoning for chicken stock (page 38)	vegetables, herbs and seasoning for chicken stock (page 38)
Farce for galantine (page 77)	Farce for galantine (page 77)	Farce for galantine (page 77)
4 oz. cooked tongue, diced	100 g. cooked tongue, diced	¾ cup diced cooked tongue
½ pint Chicken aspic jelly (page 39)	3 dl. Chicken aspic jelly (page 39)	1¼ cups Chicken aspic jelly (page 39)
¾ pint Chaudfroid sauce (page 36)	½ litre Chaudfroid sauce (page 36)	2 cups Chaudfroid sauce (page 36)
watercress or tarragon leaves, curly endive, cucumber, tomato or radishes for garnish	watercress or tarragon leaves, curly endive, cucumber, tomato or radishes for garnish	watercress or tarragon leaves, curly endive, cucumber, tomato or radishes for garnish

Bone the fowl (opposite) and set aside. Prepare the carcass, bones and giblets and put into a large pan with the knuckle of veal, chopped into 3 or 4 pieces, and the other ingredients for the chicken stock (page 38). Add 2 quarts (2¼ litres, 10 cups) cold water. Bring to the boil, skim and simmer until required.

Meanwhile, lay the boned fowl out on a board. Cover with the galantine farce and sprinkle with the diced tongue. Fold over the sides of the bird and mould it as far as possible to its original shape. Sew up the openings with coarse thread or secure with small poultry skewers laced with fine string. Wrap in a muslin cloth and tie the ends so the bird can be easily lifted in and out of the pan.

Put it into the pan, making sure the liquid covers it completely. Simmer very gently for 2–3 hours according to size and age. When tender, lift carefully from the pan. Boil up the stock, then strain, cool, remove fat and use to make the aspic jelly. Leave the chicken to cool and set overnight. If liked, it may be pressed between 2 plates with a weight on the top one.

Next day remove string and skewers. Coat evenly with cool chaudfroid sauce. Decorate with watercress or tarragon leaves, dipping each one in cool aspic jelly before putting in position. Leave to set then coat the whole bird with aspic jelly, which should be tacky but sufficiently liquid to flow evenly. Leave again to set firmly. Using a hot knife, chop up remaining jelly when set. Place the galantine on a serving dish and garnish with chopped jelly, watercress or curly endive, cucumber slices and tomato wedges or radishes.

If preferred the chaudfroid sauce may be omitted and the galantine glazed with aspic jelly only, coating twice.

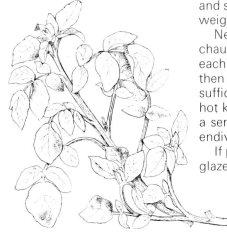

To bone and stuff chicken for a galantine (see recipe opposite)

1. Turn chicken breast downwards and slit skin down centre back of bird.

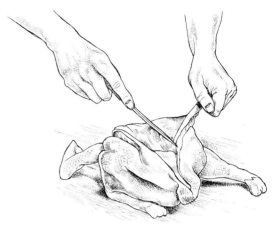

2. Work skin and flesh from carcass until thigh joint is reached. Insert knife between ball and socket of joint, sever sinew and remove thigh bone.

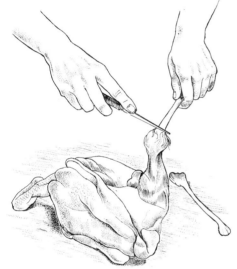

3. Hold end of joint between fingers, work meat off drumstick and remove bone completely.

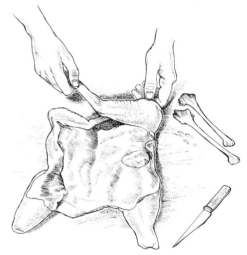

4. Sever wing joint from body and work flesh off breastbone. Repeat on other wing. Carefully ease skin off the breastbone without cutting and remove breastbone.

5. Flatten boned bird on a board and cover with the galantine farce. Sprinkle with chopped diced tongue

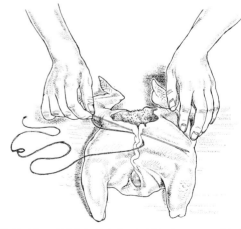

6. Fold sides of bird over and mould as far as possible back to original shape. Sew up with a trussing needle and coarse thread. Turn over and truss.

Chicken and ham mousse

Illustrated in colour on page 31
Serves 4 as a main course
or 6 as a starter

This is a super way to transform a small quantity of surplus cooked chicken, turkey or pheasant into an elegant dish, which can be served either as a starter or a main course. If larger quantities are needed, perhaps for a summer buffet party, a boiling fowl, cooked according to the recipe on page 42, would be the most economical buy.

Imperial	Metric	American
¼ pint clear chicken jelly (page 39)	1½ dl. clear chicken jelly (page 39)	⅔ cup clear chicken jelly (page 39)
½ oz. butter	15 g. butter	1 tablespoon butter
½ oz. flour	15 g. flour	2 tablespoons flour
¼ pint good chicken stock	1½ dl. good chicken stock	⅔ cup good chicken stock
1 egg, separated	1 egg, separated	1 egg, separated
3 tablespoons cream	3 tablespoons cream	scant ¼ cup cream
½ oz. powdered gelatine	15 g. powdered gelatine	2 envelopes gelatin
3 tablespoons boiling water	3 tablespoons boiling water	scant ¼ cup boiling water
6 oz. cooked chicken, minced	175 g. cooked chicken, minced	¾ cup ground cooked chicken
2 oz. cooked lean ham, minced	50 g. cooked lean ham, minced	¼ cup ground cooked lean ham
1 teaspoon tomato ketchup	1 teaspoon tomato ketchup	1 teaspoon tomato catsup
dash Worcestershire sauce	dash Worcestershire sauce	dash Worcestershire sauce
lemon juice, salt and pepper to taste	lemon juice, salt and pepper to taste	lemon juice, salt and pepper to taste
tomato, cucumber, watercress for garnish	tomato, cucumber, watercress for garnish	tomato, cucumber, watercress for garnish

Melt the chicken jelly and set aside to cool or use aspic jelly crystals according to instructions on the packet.

Make a thick white sauce (see Panada page 61) with the butter, flour and chicken stock. Beat the egg yolk and cream together and stir into the sauce. Dissolve the gelatine thoroughly in the boiling water and then stir into the sauce. Add the chicken and ham. Flavour to taste with ketchup, Worcestershire sauce, lemon juice and season well, remembering that the flavour of a chilled dish tends to be blander than a hot one.

Whisk the egg white until stiff, but not brittle, and fold the mixture carefully into it. Pour into a soufflé dish or individual ramekins, smooth the top and chill well.

When set, decorate with the garnishing vegetables in an attractive pattern: dip each piece of vegetable into the cool liquid jelly and arrange on top of the mousse. Chill until the pattern is firm, then carefully spoon over another layer of jelly and allow to set. This looks attractive and prevents the garnish from wilting.

1. Lay pattern out on a board.

2. Transfer garnish to mousse, dipping each piece of vegetable in cool liquid jelly.

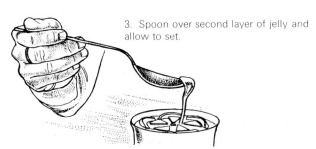

3. Spoon over second layer of jelly and allow to set.

Cold chicken with tunny sauce

Serves 6

This Italian summer dish is much easier and quicker to prepare than the classic chaudfroid of chicken. It is also an appetising way to use up surplus joints of a chicken which has been spit or oven-roasted.

Imperial	Metric	American
1 boiling or roasting chicken	1 boiling or roasting chicken	1 broiler-fryer chicken
½ pint Tunny fish mayonnaise (page 65)	3 dl. Tunny fish mayonnaise (page 65)	1¼ cups Tunny fish mayonnaise (page 65)
strained stock	strained stock	strained stock
½ cucumber or 1 small can red pimentos	½ cucumber or 1 small can red pimentos	½ cucumber or 1 small can red pimientos
curly endive or lettuce and radishes	curly endive or lettuce and radishes	curly endive or lettuce and radishes

Boil the fowl (page 42) or roast (page 9) and skin while still warm. When cold, remove the legs and separate the drumsticks and thigh joints. Carefully carve off the breast in 2 complete fillets and remove the wings, leaving the *suprêmes* (breasts). If they are large, slice each of these slant-wise in half. Make a double quantity of the recipe for Tunny fish mayonnaise and, if necessary, thin with a little strained stock. The sauce should be the consistency to coat the back of a wooden spoon evenly and fairly thickly. Place the joints on a plate, coat carefully with the sauce, and decorate with strips of cucumber or pimento. Chill the joints until set and then lift carefully on to a serving dish or individual plates. Garnish with curly endive or lettuce leaves and prepared radishes.

Serve with a salad of sliced new potatoes tossed in French dressing and garnished with chives or chopped spring onions.

Chaudfroid of chicken or pheasant

Serves 4 or 6 if using a large bird

Imperial	Metric	American
1 cooked chicken or pheasant	1 cooked chicken or pheasant	1 cooked chicken or pheasant
¾ pint Chaudfroid sauce (page 36)	scant ½ litre Chaudfroid sauce (page 36)	2 cups Chaudfroid sauce (page 36)
watercress and cucumber	watercress and cucumber	watercress and cucumber
1½ pints Chicken aspic jelly (page 39)	scant 1 litre Chicken aspic jelly (page 39)	3¾ cups Chicken aspic jelly (page 39)
salad vegetables for garnish	salad vegetables for garnish	salad vegetables for garnish

Skin and carve the cold bird as in the preceding recipe, but remove the bones from the joints and reshape. Or, leave the bird whole.

Cool the chaudfroid sauce to coating consistency, spoon evenly over the bird and leave to set.

Pull the leaves off the watercress stalks, and cut the unpeeled cucumber in thin slices and quarter. Arrange in a simple bold design of watercress sprigs and overlapping cucumber triangles on the chopping board, then transfer this on to the bird, dipping each item in the cool liquid aspic jelly before setting in position. Leave until firmly set on the sauce, then coat all over with the jelly, which is tacky but sufficiently liquid to spoon evenly over the bird. Leave to set and coat a second time if necessary.

When firmly set, arrange the bird on a serving dish and surround with remaining chopped aspic jelly. Garnish with salad vegetables.

Chaudfroid sauce ·

for coating cold bird and galantine

Make a Velouté sauce (page 60), using strained chicken stock which has set into a firm jelly and then been melted down. Cool the sauce in a bowl of cold water, stirring frequently until it is the right coating consistency for the chaudfroid dish.

Cold chicken or pheasant with green grapes

Serves 4

This delicate tasting dish is suitable for a fork lunch or supper. The bird can be boiled, oven or spit-roasted and the carcass made into the well-flavoured stock which is required.

Imperial	Metric	American
1 cooked chicken (3 lb.), pheasant or 1½ lb. cooked chicken meat	1 cooked chicken (1½ kg.), pheasant or 700 g. cooked chicken meat	1 cooked chicken (3 lb.), pheasant or 1½ lb. cooked chicken meat
2 teaspoons fresh chopped tarragon leaves or 1 teaspoon dried tarragon	2 teaspoons fresh chopped tarragon leaves or 1 teaspoon dried tarragon	2 teaspoons fresh chopped tarragon leaves or 1 teaspoon dried tarragon
½ pint good chicken stock (page 38)	3 dl. good chicken stock (page 38)	1¼ cups good chicken stock (page 38)
3 egg yolks	3 egg yolks	3 egg yolks
¼ pint double cream	1½ dl. double cream	⅔ cup heavy cream
4 fl. oz. dry white wine	1¼ dl. dry white wine	½ cup dry white wine
3–4 teaspoons lemon juice	3–4 teaspoons lemon juice	3–4 teaspoons lemon juice
salt and pepper	salt and pepper	salt and pepper
6 oz. green grapes	175 g. green grapes	⅓ lb. green grapes

Skin the chicken, remove the flesh from the bones and cut into neat pieces.

Add the tarragon to the chicken stock and boil uncovered until reduced to nearly half. Strain.

Beat the egg yolks and cream together in a bowl, stir in the wine and ¼ pint (1½ dl., ⅔ cup) of the strained stock. Place the bowl over a saucepan of simmering water, taking care that the bottom of the bowl is well clear of the water. Stir until the sauce thickens and coats the back of a wooden spoon like thin custard. Remove the bowl from the saucepan immediately or the sauce will curdle. Add the lemon juice, salt and pepper to taste.

Peel and pip the grapes and add half to the sauce with the chicken meat. Cool and pour into a shallow serving dish. Arrange the remaining grapes on top. Refrigerate until required—the sauce will gradually thicken as it chills.

Curly endive makes an attractive garnish.

Chicken and fruit curry

The following quantities are sufficient for 4 main course servings or for 6 as a first course

This is a versatile dish in which the fresh fruits can be varied according to the season. In winter, plumped dried apricots, peaches and prunes can be used and canned pineapple and mangoes if fresh are not available. The curry sauce should be spicy but mild, as a fiery sauce will kill the delicate flavours of the fruit. It also makes the dish acceptable as a starter—which must never be so pungent that the next course cannot be tasted.

Imperial	Metric	American
1 tablespoon desiccated coconut	1 tablespoon desiccated coconut	1 tablespoon shredded coconut
$\frac{1}{4}$ pint boiling water	$1\frac{1}{2}$ dl. boiling water	$\frac{2}{3}$ cup boiling water
2 small onions, finely sliced	2 small onions, finely sliced	2 small onions, finely sliced
2 oz. butter	50 g. butter	$\frac{1}{4}$ cup butter
2 tablespoons flour	2 tablespoons flour	3 tablespoons all-purpose flour
2 teaspoons curry powder	2 teaspoons curry powder	2 teaspoons curry powder
1 teaspoon curry paste	1 teaspoon curry paste	1 teaspoon curry paste
1 teaspoon crushed coriander seeds	1 teaspoon crushed coriander seeds	1 teaspoon crushed coriander seeds
2 knobs stem ginger, chopped	2 knobs stem ginger, chopped	2 knobs stem ginger, chopped
1 pint chicken stock	6 dl. chicken stock	$2\frac{1}{2}$ cups chicken stock
1 lb. prepared fruit* (see method)	450 g. prepared fruit* (see method)	1 lb. prepared fruit* (see method)
12 oz. cooked chicken meat	350 g. cooked chicken meat	$\frac{3}{4}$ lb. cooked chicken meat
5 tablespoons thick cream	5 tablespoons thick cream	6 tablespoons whipping cream
1–2 tablespoons lemon juice	1–2 tablespoons lemon juice	1–3 tablespoons lemon juice
salt to taste	salt to taste	salt to taste

*Fruits to choose are apples, pears, pineapple, apricots, peaches, prunes, bananas, tangerines, melon, mangoes.

Soak the coconut in the boiling water until required.

Fry the onions lightly in the butter. Remove from the heat and stir in the flour, curry powder and paste, coriander and ginger. Replace on the heat and continue cooking gently for 5 minutes. Blend in the strained coconut liquid and the stock and simmer for 30 minutes.

Prepare the fruit: peel, core or stone and cut into neat pieces and add. Cut the chicken into pieces and mix into the curry sauce, and then add the cream. Sharpen to taste with lemon juice and season with salt. Serve hot or ice cold.

For a first course put the chilled curry into small individual glass bowls. Stand each one in a large bowl or soup dish, surround with crushed ice, garnished with a few fresh mint leaves. Hand crisply fried poppadums separately.

For a main dish, serve with fluffy boiled rice, chappatis, nam or poppadums.

Bird in a pot

Soups

Chicken stock: Excellent stock and bouillon can be made with poultry and game. When a whole bird is boiled as described on page 42, the resulting liquor, well flavoured with its herbs and vegetables, makes a tasty and nourishing broth which can be served as a soup. The carcass from a jointed bird, together with the giblets, can be cooked into a strong bouillon or jellied stock, which makes a flavoursome base for sauces, soups and aspic jelly. The giblets, without the carcass, will produce sufficient stock to give a good flavour to gravies and sauces.

Giblet stock

To clean giblets: The giblets consist of the bird's neck, gizzard or crop, heart and liver. They must be carefully cleaned before using. The gizzard should be neatly slit round the curved outer edge and the inner sac, which contains semi-digested food, discarded. If the inner sac is broken, remove the outer skin and wash out the contents thoroughly. Remove the gall-bladder if it is still attached to the liver. If it has been broken in drawing the bird, cut off any liver that has been stained yellow as it will taste bitter. Remove surplus fat from the heart and squeeze out any blood clots under cold running water.

Imperial	Metric	American
1–2 sets cleaned giblets	1–2 sets cleaned giblets	1–2 sets cleaned giblets
1 bay leaf	1 bay leaf	1 bay leaf
1 sprig parsley	1 sprig parsley	1 sprig parsley
1 shallot (optional)	1 shallot (optional)	1 shallot (optional)
8–10 peppercorns	8–10 peppercorns	8–10 peppercorns
salt to taste	salt to taste	salt to taste
$\frac{1}{2}$–1 pint cold water	$\frac{1}{4}$–$\frac{1}{2}$ litre cold water	$1\frac{1}{4}$–$2\frac{1}{2}$ cups cold water

Put all the ingredients in a small pan, add the cold water. Cover and simmer for 20 minutes or until required.

Chicken stock or bouillon

Imperial	Metric	American
chicken carcass, skin and giblets	chicken carcass, skin and giblets	chicken carcass, skin and giblets
3–4 carrots	3–4 carrots	3–4 carrots
1 turnip	1 turnip	1 turnip
1 large onion	1 large onion	1 large onion
2–3 sticks celery	2–3 sticks celery	2–3 stalks celery
1 bay leaf	1 bay leaf	1 bay leaf
1 large sprig parsley	1 large sprig parsley	1 large sprig parsley
1 sprig rosemary	1 sprig rosemary	1 sprig rosemary
1 sprig thyme	1 sprig thyme	1 sprig thyme
6–8 peppercorns	6–8 peppercorns	6–8 peppercorns
1 teaspoon salt	1 teaspoon salt	1 teaspoon salt
2 quarts cold water	$2\frac{1}{4}$ litres cold water	5 pints cold water

Wash the chicken carcass in cold water. Prepare and clean the giblets, discarding any fat from the skin. Put all in a large saucepan. Peel and chop the vegetables and add to the pan with the herbs, pepper-corns and salt. Cover with the water. Bring slowly to the boil, skim off the scum when it rises. Cover and simmer very gently for 1 hour for a quick stock, 2 hours for a strong bouillon. For a more con-centrated bouillon, leave off the lid so that the stock reduces during cooking.

Strain, cool quickly and then remove fat by passing pieces of absorbent or tissue paper across the surface of the stock.

Chicken aspic jelly

A packet of aspic crystals can be very convenient for glazing chicken mousse, galantine and chaudfroid dishes—see Cold bird section. On the other hand, the more flavoursome homemade jelly is an essential ingredient for the Raised game or chicken pie (page 26).

For the pie, jellied chicken or game bouillon made from the carcass and giblets, reduced until it jells naturally and then melted and strained, may be used without further preparation. However, for dishes which require a crystal clear jelly, the bouillon must be cleared before setting by the addition of egg whites and shells and very lean beef, which contain the essential albumen.

To clear a bouillon

Imperial	Metric	American
2 pints jellied chicken bouillon	generous 1 litre jellied chicken bouillon	5 cups jellied chicken bouillon
6 oz. lean shin of beef, minced	175 g. lean shin of beef, minced	$\frac{3}{4}$ cup ground lean beef shank
2 fl. oz. dry sherry	4 tablespoons dry sherry	$\frac{1}{3}$ cup dry sherry
2 egg whites	2 egg whites	2 egg whites
2 egg shells	2 egg shells	2 egg shells
salt and pepper	salt and pepper	salt and pepper
lemon juice for flavouring	lemon juice for flavouring	lemon juice for flavoring

Carefully remove any grease from the bouillon by straining it through a cold wet cloth into an enamel-lined saucepan. Add the meat and sherry. Whip the egg whites to a soft froth and add to the pan with the crushed egg shells. Continue whisking over a moderate heat until the bouillon comes to the boil. Stop whisking and allow the froth to rise to the top of the saucepan. Draw aside and leave the crust to settle, then boil up again slowly so the crust does not break. Scald a clean cloth and line a large strainer placed over a bowl. When the bouillon has settled for 7–10 minutes, pour into the strainer, holding back the frothy crust with a large draining spoon until the end, then allow it to slide into the strainer. Move the strainer to another bowl and pour the bouillon carefully through the frothy filter a second time. Season the liquid jelly and flavour to taste with lemon juice.

Scots chicken and almond soup— Feather fowlie

Serves 6–8

This rich and satisfying soup, a favourite of Mary Queen of Scots, has a delicate flavour of almonds and cream.

Imperial	Metric	American
1 small boiling fowl	1 small boiling fowl	1 small stewing chicken
2 medium onions	2 medium onions	2 medium onions
1 turnip	1 turnip	1 turnip
1 parsnip	1 parsnip	1 parsnip
3–4 carrots	3–4 carrots	3–4 carrots
3 sticks celery	3 sticks celery	3 stalks celery
1 bay leaf	1 bay leaf	1 bay leaf
1 sprig each parsley and thyme	1 sprig each parsley and thyme	1 sprig each parsley and thyme
10 peppercorns	10 peppercorns	10 peppercorns
salt	salt	salt
2 oz. ground almonds	50 g. ground almonds	$\frac{1}{2}$ cup ground almonds
3 tablespoons fresh white breadcrumbs	3 tablespoons fresh white breadcrumbs	scant $\frac{1}{4}$ cup fresh white bread crumbs
$\frac{1}{4}$ pint double cream	$1\frac{1}{2}$ dl. double cream	$\frac{2}{3}$ cup whipping cream
2 tablespoons snipped chives or chopped parsley for garnish	2 tablespoons snipped chives or chopped parsley for garnish	3 tablespoons snipped chives or chopped parsley for garnish

Put the trussed fowl with the cleaned giblets in a large saucepan. Cover with cold water. Clean, peel and chop the vegetables and add with the herbs and seasonings to the pan. Bring quickly to the boil. Reduce the heat and skim carefully. Continue to simmer slowly for 2 hours or until the fowl is very tender.

Lift it out of the pan and remove the flesh from the bones. Put the meat in a blender. Strain the stock, set the giblets and herbs aside; add the vegetables to the blender with a little of the stock and make into a purée. Alternatively put the meat and vegetables through a fine mincer. Turn the purée back into the saucepan, stir in the ground almonds and breadcrumbs and about 2 pints (1 litre, 5 cups) of strained chicken stock.

Simmer for 15–20 minutes. Mix a cup of soup into the cream and stir this mixture into the soup. Heat without boiling and serve sprinkled with snipped chives or chopped parsley.

Avgolémono

Serves 6

This traditional Greek chicken and lemon soup is very simple to make. It has a pleasant refreshing taste so it is an attractive choice for summer days.

Imperial	Metric	American
2 pints good chicken stock	generous 1 litre good chicken stock	5 cups good chicken stock
2 oz. rice	50 g. rice	generous $\frac{1}{3}$ cup rice
1 large or 2 small lemons	1 large or 2 small lemons	1 large or 2 small lemons
2 eggs	2 eggs	2 eggs
chopped fresh mint for garnish	chopped fresh mint for garnish	chopped fresh mint for garnish

Strain the chicken stock and bring to the simmer. Add the rice and cook for 20 minutes. Squeeze the juice from the lemons and beat together with the eggs. Gradually blend in a cupful of chicken stock, then stir this mixture back into the pan. Heat the soup but do not allow it to boil. Serve sprinkled with chopped mint.

Cream of chicken soup

Serves 6–8

This creamy soup is equally suitable for a family meal or a lunch or dinner party.

Imperial	Metric	American
1 pint good chicken stock	generous ½ litre good chicken stock	2½ cups good chicken stock
1 pint Blanquette sauce (page 61)	generous ½ litre Blanquette sauce (page 61)	2½ cups Blanquette sauce (page 61)
1 tablespoon chopped chives	1 tablespoon chopped chives	1 tablespoon chopped chives
2 tablespoons chopped parsley	2 tablespoons chopped parsley	3 tablespoons chopped parsley
¼ pint cream	1½ dl. cream	⅔ cup cream
salt, pepper and lemon juice	salt, pepper and lemon juice	salt, pepper and lemon juice
croûtons for garnish	croûtons for garnish	croûtons for garnish

Remove any bones and giblets from the stock, but leave in the vegetables. Heat the Blanquette sauce in a large pan and gradually blend in the chicken stock. Bring to the simmer and cook gently for 30 minutes stirring frequently.

Strain into a large bowl. Push the vegetables through a sieve with a wooden spoon or put into a blender with a little stock to make a purée. Put the soup and vegetable purée back into the pan, add the chives and parsley and bring to the simmer. Mix a little soup into the cream and stir this mixture into the soup. Heat through, but do not boil. Adjust the seasoning and sharpen to taste with lemon juice.

Serve hot with bread croûtons, crisply fried in butter.

Petite marmite

Illustrated in colour on the jacket
Serves 6–8

This French soup is named after the little brown pots, like individual casseroles, in which it is traditionally served. The vegetables can be cut in fine Julienne strips, shredded or chopped.

Imperial	Metric	American
2 pints good chicken stock	generous 1 litre good chicken stock	5 cups good chicken stock
1 leek	1 leek	1 leek
2 tablespoons shredded or chopped carrot	2 tablespoons shredded or chopped carrot	3 tablespoons shredded or chopped carrot
2 tablespoons shredded or chopped young turnip	2 tablespoons shredded or chopped young turnip	3 tablespoons shredded or chopped young turnip
2 tablespoons shredded cabbage heart	2 tablespoons shredded cabbage heart	3 tablespoons shredded cabbage heart
2 tablespoons shredded or chopped, cooked chicken meat	2 tablespoons shredded or chopped, cooked chicken meat	3 tablespoons shredded or chopped, cooked chicken meat
seasoning	seasoning	seasoning
chopped parsley and croûtons for garnish	chopped parsley and croûtons for garnish	chopped parsley and croûtons for garnish

Strain the chicken stock and skim off the fat. Cut off the white part of the leek, clean it and slice it very finely. Bring the stock to the boil and add the leek, carrot, turnip and cabbage. Simmer for 15 minutes, add the shredded chicken and cook for a further 5 minutes. Adjust seasoning and garnish with chopped parsley.

Serve in a tureen or individual soup bowls with croûtons or a bowl of grated Parmesan cheese.

Boiled fowl

Birds which are too old to roast, grill or fry can be made into a variety of attractive dishes by simmering slowly in a well seasoned stock, flavoured with vegetables and herbs.

The surplus fat round the vent and any eggs should first be removed and the breast rubbed with lemon juice to keep it white. Truss the fowl as for roasting (page 9). If it is not much over a year old it will be cooked in about $1\frac{1}{4}$ hours, but if it is a large farmyard fowl weighing about 5 lb. ($2\frac{1}{4}$ kg.) it will take 2 hours or more.

Boiled chicken with rice and parsley sauce

Serves 6–8

Imperial	Metric	American
1 boiling fowl (4–5 lb.)	1 boiling fowl ($1\frac{3}{4}$–$2\frac{1}{4}$ kg.)	1 stewing chicken (4–5 lb.)
lemon juice	lemon juice	lemon juice
12 button onions, peeled	12 button onions, peeled	12 tiny onions, peeled
2–3 sticks celery, chopped	2–3 sticks celery, chopped	2–3 stalks celery, chopped
1 lb. small carrots, scraped	$\frac{1}{2}$ kg. small carrots, scraped	1 lb. small carrots, cleaned
2 bay leaves	2 bay leaves	2 bay leaves
1 large sprig parsley	1 large sprig parsley	1 large sprig parsley
1 sprig thyme or rosemary	1 sprig thyme or rosemary	1 sprig thyme or rosemary
8 peppercorns	8 peppercorns	8 peppercorns
salt	salt	salt
4 oz. belly pork, salted or fresh	100 g. belly pork, salted or fresh	$\frac{1}{4}$ lb. fresh picnic shoulder pork or salt pork
12 oz. rice	350 g. rice	$1\frac{2}{3}$ cups rice
$\frac{3}{4}$ pint Parsley sauce (page 60)	$\frac{1}{2}$ litre Parsley sauce (page 60)	2 cups Parsley sauce (page 60)
chopped parsley for garnish	chopped parsley for garnish	chopped parsley for garnish

Prepare the fowl (above) and giblets for boiling. Half fill a large saucepan with water, add the vegetables, herbs and seasoning. Bring to the boil. Put in the giblets and fowl, breast uppermost, and make sure the legs are covered by water. Remove the rind from the pork, cut into 2-inch (5-cm.) chunks and add to the pot. Cover and simmer very gently for $\frac{1}{2}$ hour, then turn the bird on one side for 20 minutes, and then the other side. Continue simmering until the legs are tender. When cooked, lift it out of the pot, cover with a cloth and keep warm.

Strain the stock into a cold bowl and set aside the pork and vegetables. Skim off as much fat as possible and remove the remainder with absorbent or tissue paper. Pour the stock back into the saucepan, retaining $\frac{1}{2}$ pint (3 dl., $1\frac{1}{4}$ cups) for sauce, bring to the boil and add the rice. Cook for 12–14 minutes until only just tender, then strain into a colander or sieve and cover with a dry cloth to keep warm.

Meanwhile, make the Parsley sauce using $\frac{1}{2}$ pint (3 dl., $1\frac{1}{4}$ cups) of the strained chicken stock.

To serve: place the fowl on a carving plate with the pieces of pork and onions and garnish with parsley. Slice the carrots, toss in butter with cooked peas or chopped green beans and place on a warmed vegetable dish. Serve the rice and parsley sauce in separate bowls.

Blanquette of chicken

Serves 4

This French dish is a party version of Boiled chicken with rice. It is a carefree dish for the cook/hostess as it can easily be prepared in advance and all you need is 15 minutes to cook the rice for the border.

Imperial	Metric	American
1 small boiling fowl	1 small boiling fowl	1 small stewing chicken
1 onion	1 onion	1 onion
3–4 carrots, sliced	3–4 carrots, sliced	3–4 carrots, sliced
1 stick celery	1 stick celery	1 stalk celery
1 bay leaf	1 bay leaf	1 bay leaf
1 large sprig parsley	1 large sprig parsley	1 large sprig parsley
salt and pepper	salt and pepper	salt and pepper
1 pint Blanquette sauce (page 61)	generous ½ litre Blanquette sauce (page 61)	2½ cups Blanquette sauce (page 61)
8 oz. rice	225 g. rice	generous 1 cup rice
mushroom caps and parsley sprigs for garnish	mushroom caps and parsley sprigs for garnish	mushroom caps and parsley sprigs for garnish

Prepare the fowl for boiling (page 42). (If in a hurry, the bird may be divided into joints and these will cook very much quicker than the whole bird.) Put in a saucepan with the vegetables, herbs and seasoning, cover with hot water. Bring rapidly to the boil, then lower heat. Cover and simmer very gently until the legs are tender.

Lift out the chicken, skin and divide into joints if whole. Strain the stock and measure ½ pint (3 dl., 1¼ cups) to make blanquette sauce. When the sauce is ready, add the chicken joints and heat through. Adjust seasoning.

Meanwhile, cook the rice in the remaining stock for 12 minutes or until just tender. Strain into a colander and dry under a cloth.

Arrange the rice into a border around a warmed serving dish and put the chicken and sauce in the centre. Garnish the border with carrot slices from the stock, fried mushroom caps and parsley sprigs.

Cock-a-leekie

This traditional Scottish crofter's dish is cooked like Boiled chicken with rice but using 1 lb. (½ kg.) leeks instead of carrots, pearl barley instead of the rice and a few prunes for flavour. Sometimes the flesh is removed from the bones when the fowl is cooked and served in the soup like French *pot-au-feu*, but usually the soup and chicken are served separately with a lemon or parsley sauce.

Boiley-bakey chicken

This is a less expensive alternative to roast chicken.

Boil the fowl in a well flavoured stock until nearly tender, but not completely cooked, and remove from the pot. Drain well and pat the outside dry with absorbent paper. Put 2–3 oz. (50–75 g.) lard in a roasting pan and heat it in a hot oven (425°F, 220°C, Gas Mark 7). Put in the fowl and baste with the hot fat. Roast for 20–30 minutes, according to size, basting frequently, until golden brown and the legs are tender.

Chipolata sausages can be roasted round the bird to make a tasty garnish.

Bird in a casserole

Casserole cooking, long a favourite method in peasant families throughout Europe, has become increasingly popular.

It is particularly suitable for tenderising older birds and is a very convenient method for the cook who is a single-handed hostess, or has a very unpunctual family, as food can be kept warm while waiting without spoiling.

Earthenware and ovenproof glass are inexpensive, but they cannot be used on a naked flame. Some of them can be put on a special type of heat-diffusing mat over a very low heat, but they are really safest in the oven. Meat or poultry, which has to be browned before liquid is added, must be cooked in a frying pan and then transferred to the casserole.

Flameproof casseroles made of 'rocket glass' or metal are more expensive, but are also much more versatile, being three pots in one. They can be used on top of the stove to sauté meat and make sauces, then left to simmer gently over a low heat or transferred to a slow oven. Many are so attractively finished that they can be placed on the table for serving. This all saves time and labour, especially if the lining is non-stick teflon.

Pot roasting is suitable for cooking a bird whole, and a flameproof, deep oval casserole is the best shape to use. The chicken or game is first browned all over in hot fat, with one or two whole onions spiked with cloves. A glass of wine or stock is then added with herbs and seasoning. A close fitting lid is put on and the bird left to cook very slowly over a low flame, allowing about 30 minutes per pound ($\frac{1}{2}$ kg.). When the bird is cooked, the onion is discarded, surplus fat removed from the casserole and the juices served as gravy, which may be slightly thickened and extended with stock as in oven roasting.

Casseroled bird in sauce: for these dishes the bird is usually divided into joints and these are first sautéed in hot fat before vegetables and liquid are added. A flameproof casserole, which is fairly shallow and wide enough to fry several joints, is best.

Sauté pans are wide shallow saucepans with a lid, and are also suitable for cooking jointed birds. They are aluminium, stainless steel or iron and the best are lined with enamel or non-stick teflon. If the pan has a long handle, cooking will have to be confined to the top of the stove, but if it has small heatproof handles, cooking can be completed in the oven.

In addition to the following recipes, other interesting casserole dishes are found in Foreign and exotic birds section (page 52).

West Country chicken with cider

Serves 4

This favourite West Country dish with its apples, cider and cream is equally successful with guinea fowl or pheasant. If the game is not a roasting bird, it will need longer cooking before the cream is added.

The meat from the carcass, giblets and stock will make a tasty Risotto (page 70) the next day.

Imperial	Metric	American
1 oven-ready chicken (3½ lb.)	1 oven-ready chicken (1½ kg.)	1 ready-to-cook chicken (3½ lb.)
giblet stock ingredients (page 38)	giblet stock ingredients (page 38)	giblet stock ingredients (page 38)
2 oz. flour	50 g. flour	½ cup all-purpose flour
3 oz. unsalted butter	75 g. unsalted butter	6 tablespoons sweet butter
1 large onion, thinly sliced	1 large onion, thinly sliced	1 large onion, thinly sliced
1–2 sticks celery, chopped	1–2 sticks celery, chopped	1–2 stalks celery, chopped
1 large or 2 small cooking apples	1 large or 2 small cooking apples	1 large or 2 small baking apples
¼ pint dry cider	1½ dl. dry cider	⅔ cup cider
½ pint giblet stock	3 dl. giblet stock	1¼ cups giblet stock
4 tablespoons thick cream	4 tablespoons thick cream	⅓ cup whipping cream
salt and pepper	salt and pepper	salt and pepper
1 dessert apple and celery leaves for garnish	1 dessert apple and celery leaves for garnish	1 eating apple and celery leaves for garnish

Joint (page 46) and skin the chicken. Put the carcass, skin and giblets in a saucepan with the other stock ingredients. Cover and simmer until required.

Flour the chicken joints and fry them until golden in 2 oz. (50 g.) of the butter in a flameproof casserole or sauté pan. Remove, put in the onion and celery and fry gently until softened. Peel and coarsely chop the apple. Add to the pan and cook for a few minutes until well buttered. Draw the pan from the heat and stir in enough flour (about 3 tablespoons) to absorb the fat. Gradually stir in the cider and giblet stock. Bring to the simmer, add the chicken and if necessary a little more stock to cover the joints. Put on the lid and simmer over a low heat for 30 minutes or until the bird is tender. When cooked, remove the chicken, cook the sauce briskly without a lid for 5 minutes or until slightly thickened. Mix 2–3 tablespoons of sauce into the cream and stir this mixture into the pan. Adjust seasoning.

Arrange the chicken joints in a warmed deep serving dish and pour over the sauce. Core the unpeeled dessert apple and cut into thick slices. Heat the remaining butter in a frying pan and fry the apple rings briskly until golden brown, turning once. Arrange the rings at each end of the dish and push a little tuft of celery leaves through each ring.

Serving suggestions:

Accompany with new potatoes tossed with butter and parsley, or Duchesse potatoes, and buttered broccoli spears or tiny Brussels sprouts.

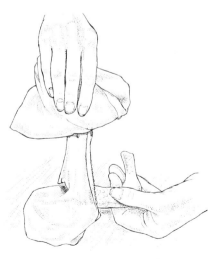

Grasp chicken joint firmly in one hand and pull skin off with the other, using a cloth to grip with.

Normandy pheasant

The bird is prepared and cooked as in the recipe for West Country chicken with cider, but is given extra dash by the addition of flaming Calvados, the famous Normandy apple brandy.

After the joints have been fried, surplus fat is removed and 1–2 tablespoons of Calvados are warmed in a little pan, set alight and poured flaming over the bird. When the flames have subsided, the joints are removed, the onion and celery are added with the butter, and the recipe continued. Guinea fowl and chicken are also excellent prepared in this manner and it is strongly recommended for frozen birds.

To joint a chicken

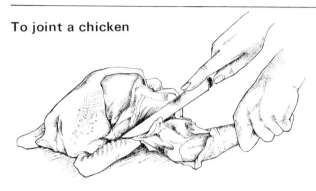

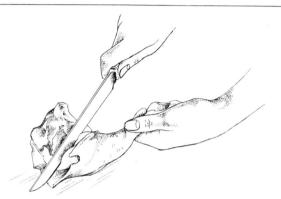

1. Insert knife between leg and body and cut down through skin to thigh joint. Take leg in other hand and dislocate thick joint by pressing leg backwards. Insert knife between ball and socket of joint. Separate leg from bird.

2. Divide thigh and drumstick in similar manner.

3. Remove wing joints

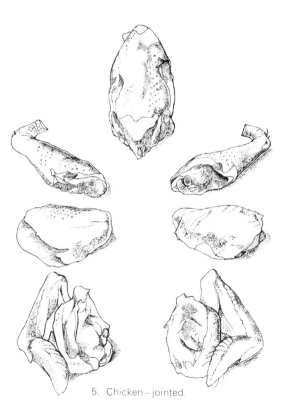

4. Cut along rib cage with knife or scissors on both sides of bird, separating breast from back. Divide breast into two halves by cutting down one side of breastbone.

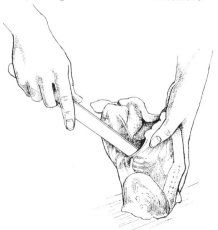

5. Chicken—jointed.

Coq au vin de Bourgogne

Serves 4

This is one of the chicken dishes which most often appears on restaurant menus but, sadly, frequently turns out to be indifferently stewed chicken instead of the rich Burgundian casserole of its country of origin. In this traditional recipe, the bird is cooked whole, but it may be jointed if preferred. If pickled pork is not available, green streaky bacon may be used.

Imperial	Metric	American
giblet stock ingredients (page 38)	giblet stock ingredients (page 38)	giblet stock ingredients (page 38)
3 oz. unsalted butter	75 g. unsalted butter	6 tablespoons sweet butter
4 oz. pickled belly pork, diced	100 g. pickled belly pork, diced	$\frac{2}{3}$ cup diced salt pork
12 button onions	12 button onions	12 tiny onions
6–8 oz. button mushrooms	175–225 g. button mushrooms	$1\frac{1}{2}$–2 cups button mushrooms
1 young cockerel or chicken	1 young cockerel or chicken	1 broiler-fryer chicken
1 tablespoon brandy	1 tablespoon brandy	1 tablespoon brandy
$\frac{1}{2}$–$\frac{3}{4}$ bottle Burgundy or dry red wine	$\frac{1}{2}$–$\frac{3}{4}$ bottle Burgundy or dry red wine	$\frac{1}{2}$–$\frac{3}{4}$ bottle Burgundy or dry red wine
bouquet garni or 1 teaspoon crushed dried herbs	bouquet garni or 1 teaspoon crushed dried herbs	bouquet garni or 1 teaspoon crushed dried herbs
1 clove garlic	1 clove garlic	1 clove garlic
salt and black pepper	salt and black pepper	salt and black pepper
chopped parsley and croûtons for garnish	chopped parsley and croûtons for garnish	chopped parsley and croûtons for garnish
beurre manié:	*beurre manié:*	*beurre manié:*
1 oz. butter	25 g. butter	2 tablespoons butter
1 oz. flour	25 g. flour	$\frac{1}{4}$ cup flour

Put the giblet stock ingredients on to cook and reduce into a well-flavoured bouillon.

Heat the butter in a flameproof casserole with the pickled pork and cook gently until the fat runs. Add the peeled onions and fry until golden. Wash and add the mushrooms, and cook for a few minutes. Remove all from the pan and brown the bird all over, turning carefully. Spoon out surplus fat. Warm the brandy in a tiny saucepan or large spoon, set alight and pour it flaming over the bird. Move the bird about until the flames subside, then pour in the wine.

Add the herbs and pressed garlic, the onions and mushrooms. Strain in sufficient giblet stock so that the bird is half covered. Put on the lid and simmer very gently until the legs are tender, turning the bird from time to time.

When cooked, remove the bird to a heated serving dish. Surround with the onions and mushrooms and keep warm.

Leave the sauce boiling briskly, uncovered, to reduce. Meanwhile, cream together the butter and flour and roll into little balls of *beurre manié*. Turn down the heat under the casserole, remove the bouquet garni and gradually stir in the *beurre manié* until the sauce is of the desired consistency. Season and pour into a warmed sauce boat.

Sprinkle the chicken with chopped parsley and garnish.

Serving suggestions:
The Coq may be jointed, before serving, and the sauce poured over.

Accompany with creamed or Duchesse potatoes and Brussels sprouts, or runner beans cooked French style, not sliced.

Chicken with lemon and artichokes

Serves 4

The fresh lemons combined with the subtle flavour of the artichokes give this dish its unique appeal. Unless you live in a country where fresh globe artichokes are prolific and cheap, the canned *fonds* (bottoms) may be preferred. Sometimes canned hearts are easier to come by and may be substituted if necessary.

Imperial	Metric	American
1 roasting chicken (3½ lb.)	1 roasting chicken (1½ kg.)	1 roaster chicken (3½ lb.)
2 oz. seasoned flour	50 g. seasoned flour	½ cup seasoned flour
2 oz. butter	50 g. butter	¼ cup butter
1 tablespoon chopped onion	1 tablespoon chopped onion	1 tablespoon chopped onion
4 fresh artichoke bottoms or 1 (12 oz.) can artichoke bottoms	4 fresh artichoke bottoms or 1 (350 g.) can artichoke bottoms	4 fresh artichoke bottoms or 1 (12 oz.) can artichoke bottoms
4 fl. oz. white wine	1¼ dl. white wine	6–7 tablespoons white wine
2 small or 1 large lemon	2 small or 1 large lemon	2 small or 1 large lemon
¾ pint giblet stock or bouillon	½ litre giblet stock or bouillon	2 cups giblet stock or bouillon
¼ pint double cream	1½ dl. double cream	⅔ cup whipping cream
salt and pepper	salt and pepper	salt and pepper

Joint the chicken (page 46) and put the carcass and giblets to cook to make stock (page 38).

Coat the chicken with flour. Pat off surplus and fry in a flameproof casserole in hot butter, turning once, until golden brown. Add the onion and fresh artichoke bottoms—halve if large—and the wine. (If using canned artichokes, add here with the liquor from the can and reduce the quantity of giblet stock accordingly.) Grate the zest (yellow rind without pith) off 1 small lemon or ½ a large one and add to the pan with the juice. Pour in sufficient stock or bouillon to cover the chicken joints. Put on the lid and simmer very gently for 40 minutes or until legs are tender.

Mix a few tablespoons of sauce with the cream and stir this into the pan. Adjust the seasoning and add more lemon juice if liked.

Heat through and garnish with lemon butterflies or zest, and serve with new potatoes or noodles tossed with butter and fresh parsley.

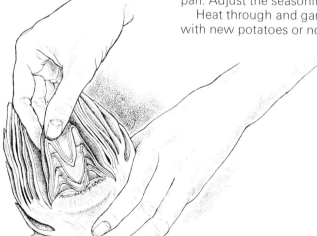

1. To prepare a cooked artichoke, open up artichoke and pull out small centre leaves with fingers

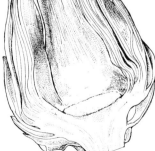

2. Remove hairy choke with a spoon, exposing the edible *fond* (bottom); discard outer leaves

Flemish chicken with chicory and prunes

Serves 4

The Belgians are great growers of chicory, which is often called Belgian endive, as in French its name is endive. Confusion can be caused by the fact that the curly salad vegetable called endive in English-speaking countries, is known as chicory on the Continent. No matter what it is called, it is equally good raw in a salad or cooked as in this recipe, when its slightly sharp taste is softened by the sweetness of the prunes. A pheasant, rather too long in the claw to roast, is very tasty cooked in this way.

Imperial	Metric	American
1 (2½ lb.) chicken or pheasant	1 (1¼ kg.) chicken or pheasant	1 (2½ lb.) chicken or pheasant
4 medium chicory heads	4 medium chicory heads	4 medium Belgian endive heads
8 oz. ripe tomatoes or 1 small can peeled tomatoes	225 g. ripe tomatoes or 1 small can peeled tomatoes	½ lb. ripe tomatoes or 1 small can peeled tomatoes
1 oz. butter	25 g. butter	2 tablespoons butter
1 tablespoon olive oil	1 tablespoon olive oil	1 tablespoon olive oil
1 medium onion, sliced	1 medium onion, sliced	1 medium onion, sliced
2 oz. belly pork or bacon	50 g. belly pork or bacon	2 oz. bacon or salt pork
3–4 tablespoons sherry	3–4 tablespoons sherry	4–5 tablespoons sherry
¼ teaspoon mixed dried herbs	¼ teaspoon mixed dried herbs	¼ teaspoon mixed dried herbs
salt and pepper	salt and pepper	salt and pepper
8 large prunes	8 large prunes	8 large prunes
¾ pint chicken stock	½ litre chicken stock	2 cups chicken stock
4 tablespoons cream (optional)	4 tablespoons cream (optional)	⅓ cup cream (optional)

Joint the bird (page 46) and put the carcass and giblets on to cook to make stock (page 38).

Trim the base of the chicory heads and remove any discoloured leaves. Skin the tomatoes and chop roughly. Heat the butter and oil in a flameproof casserole and fry the chicory until golden brown all over. Remove them and brown the chicken joints. Remove and fry the onion and pork or bacon until just colouring. Mix in the tomatoes, sherry, herbs and seasoning. Add the chicken, chicory and prunes and sufficient chicken stock to almost cover the bird. Cover and simmer gently on top of the stove or in a slow oven (325°F, 170°C, Gas Mark 3) for 1½ hours or until tender.

Arrange the chicken joints, chicory heads and stoned prunes on a warm serving dish. If using cream, stir this into the casserole. Adjust the seasoning, heat through and pour over the joints. Serve with Scalloped potatoes which will cook very conveniently in the oven at the same time as the casserole.

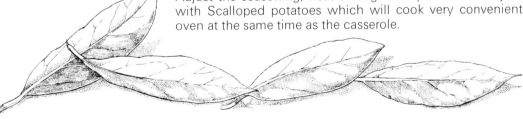

Scalloped potatoes

Well butter a shallow gratin dish and fill with layers of sliced potatoes (1 lb., ½ kg.), seasoned with salt and pepper and sprinkled with finely chopped onion and grated cheese. Beat an egg into ½ pint (3 dl., 1¼ cups) milk and pour this over the potatoes. Dot the top layer of grated cheese with butter and bake in a moderate oven (325°F, 170°C, Gas Mark 3) for 1½ hours or until cooked and golden.

Chicken livers de luxe

Nowadays chicken livers can conveniently be bought in packs of 8 oz. (225 g.) or 1 lb. (450 g.).

The livers should always be carefully cleaned and never overcooked or these tender morsels will become hard.

Chicken liver kebabs

Illustrated in colour opposite
Serves 1

Imperial	Metric	American
for each skewer:	*for each skewer:*	*for each skewer:*
1 chicken liver, cleaned	1 chicken liver, cleaned	1 chicken liver, cleaned
½ oz. butter	15 g. butter	1 tablespoon butter
1–2 bacon rolls	1–2 bacon rolls	1–2 bacon rolls
2 mushroom caps	2 mushroom caps	2 mushroom caps
1 wedge green pepper	1 wedge green pepper	1 wedge green sweet pepper
1 wedge red pepper	1 wedge red pepper	1 wedge red sweet pepper
1–2 cocktail sausages	1–2 cocktail sausages	1–2 cocktail sausages
1–2 button onions, boiled	1–2 button onions, boiled	1–2 tiny onions, boiled
1 wedge pineapple	1 wedge pineapple	1 wedge pineapple
oil for brushing	oil for brushing	oil for brushing
salt and pepper	salt and pepper	salt and pepper
dried mixed herbs	dried mixed herbs	dried mixed herbs

Sauté the halved chicken liver in butter until just stiffened. Thread the ingredients on to the skewer, alternating the colours. Brush with oil, season well and sprinkle with herbs. Grill on the stove or over a charcoal grill, turning frequently for about 10 minutes.

Chicken liver crostini

Serves 4

Imperial	Metric	American
8 oz. chicken livers	225 g. chicken livers	½ lb. chicken livers
1½ oz. butter	40 g. butter	3 tablespoons butter
4 oz. ham, diced	100 g. ham, diced	½ cup diced cooked ham
2–3 tablespoons seasoned flour	2–3 tablespoons seasoned flour	3–4 tablespoons seasoned flour
2 tablespoons sherry	2 tablespoons sherry	3 tablespoons sherry
4 tablespoons chicken stock	4 tablespoons chicken stock	⅓ cup chicken stock
4 slices white bread	4 slices white bread	4 slices white bread
butter or oil	butter or oil	butter or oil
4 tablespoons cream	4 tablespoons cream	⅓ cup cream
salt, pepper, lemon juice	salt, pepper, lemon juice	salt, pepper, lemon juice

Cut the cleaned chicken livers into neat pieces. Heat the butter in a saucepan and fry the ham quickly. Coat each piece of chicken liver in the seasoned flour, add to the pan and fry for 2 or 3 minutes until stiffened. Add sherry and stock, cook gently for 8–10 minutes.

Meanwhile, cut a round out of each bread slice and fry quickly on each side in the hot butter or oil in a frying pan. Drain on soft absorbent paper before placing on serving dishes. Add the cream to the livers, season and sharpen to taste with lemon. Pile on to croutons, sprinkle with grated lemon rind and parsley, serve at once.

Foreign and exotic birds

Persian chicken

Serves 2

In the Middle East the average chicken works so hard to find its food, it is neither large nor plump; but recipes for cooking it often contain intriguing fruits and spices. For the following dish the apricots, peaches and prunes should be soaked overnight and the liquor reserved.

Imperial	Metric	American
2 poussins or 1 spring chicken	2 poussins or 1 spring chicken	2 small or 1 large broiler chicken
2 tablespoons olive oil	2 tablespoons olive oil	3 tablespoons olive oil
2 medium onions, sliced	2 medium onions, sliced	2 medium onions, sliced
2 oz. dried apricots, plumped	50 g. dried apricots, plumped	$\frac{1}{3}$ cup dried apricots, plumped
2 oz. dried peaches, plumped	50 g. dried peaches, plumped	$\frac{1}{3}$ cup dried peaches, plumped
4 stoned prunes, plumped	4 stoned prunes, plumped	4 pitted prunes, plumped
grated rind and juice 1 orange	grated rind and juice 1 orange	grated rind and juice 1 orange
1 sharp apple	1 sharp apple	1 sharp apple
2 tablespoons seedless raisins	2 tablespoons seedless raisins	3 tablespoons seedless raisins
$\frac{1}{4}$ teaspoon cinnamon	$\frac{1}{4}$ teaspoon cinnamon	$\frac{1}{4}$ teaspoon cinnamon
pinch ginger or saffron	pinch ginger or saffron	pinch ginger or saffron
salt, pepper and lemon juice to taste	salt, pepper and lemon juice to taste	salt, pepper and lemon juice to taste

Truss the birds neatly (page 9). Heat the oil in a flameproof casserole. Brown the chickens all over and remove. Fry the onion gently until softened and just turning colour. Drain the apricots, peaches (quarter if large) and prunes and mix with the onions. Put back the chickens, add the orange rind and juice and sufficient liquor from the plumped fruits to come half way up the birds. Add the apple, peeled and thickly sliced, raisins, cinnamon, ginger or saffron and season to taste. Cover and simmer for 45 minutes or until tender, turning the birds from time to time. Sharpen the sauce with lemon juice and adjust the seasoning.

Serving suggestions:
Serve with fluffy boiled rice tossed with fried almond flakes or chopped walnuts, and with baked courgettes or aubergines.

Spiced Bangkok chicken

Serves 6–8

This Indo-Chinese dish is excellent for a buffet party as it is easy to serve at a help-yourself meal or fork luncheon, either as a main course or starter. The cumin and coriander seeds and peanut butter give the rice an intriguing flavour.

Imperial	Metric	American
1 dressed boiling fowl (4 lb.)	1 dressed boiling fowl (1¾ kg.)	1 ready-to-cook stewing chicken (4 lb.)
1 lb. onions	½ kg. onions	1 lb. onions
1 bay leaf	1 bay leaf	1 bay leaf
sprig parsley	sprig parsley	sprig parsley
salt and black pepper	salt and black pepper	salt and black pepper
1 lb. rice	450 g. rice	2⅓ cups rice
3 tablespoons vegetable oil	3 tablespoons vegetable oil	scant ¼ cup vegetable oil
2 tablespoons peanut butter	2 tablespoons peanut butter	3 tablespoons peanut butter
½ teaspoon chilli powder	½ teaspoon chilli powder	½ teaspoon chili powder
6 oz. cooked ham, diced	175 g. cooked ham, diced	1 cup diced cooked ham
1 teaspoon cumin seeds	1 teaspoon cumin seeds	1 teaspoon cumin seeds
1½ teaspoons coriander seeds	1½ teaspoons coriander seeds	1½ teaspoons coriander seeds
1 clove garlic	1 clove garlic	1 clove garlic
pinch ground mace or nutmeg	pinch ground mace or nutmeg	pinch ground mace or nutmeg
cucumber, pineapple and lemon for garnish	cucumber, pineapple and lemon for garnish	cucumber, pineapple and lemon for garnish

Simmer the fowl until tender with 1 peeled onion, the bay leaf, parsley and salt and pepper to taste. Lift out the fowl and remove the meat from the bones.

Strain and reheat the stock, add the rice and cook until just tender. Drain through a colander and cover with a dry cloth.

Peel and slice the remaining onions. Heat the oil in a large frying pan and fry the onions slowly until beginning to colour. Stir in the peanut butter, chilli powder, ham and chicken meat and then the rice, which should be dry and fluffy. Continue stirring and frying until the rice is slightly brown. Crush the cumin and coriander seeds and garlic and stir them, with the mace, into the rice. Season to taste with salt.

Pile on a hot dish and garnish with sliced unpeeled cucumber and wedges of fresh pineapple and lemon.

Serving suggestions:
Surround the serving dish with little bowls containing various chutneys such as apricot, lemon and mango, and dishes of fried almonds, cashew nuts and toasted coconut.

Hungarian chicken paprikash

Illustrated in colour opposite
Serves 4

This is a party version of the famous Hungarian chicken dish.

Paprika is a red pepper made from pimentos or sweet peppers and is not to be confused with the fiery hot cayenne pepper. It varies in strength and sufficient should be used to give the rosy pink sauce a distinctive paprika, not tomato, flavour. If single cream is used instead of soured cream, the sauce will need sharpening well with lemon juice.

Imperial	Metric	American
1 roasting chicken ($3\frac{1}{2}$ lb.)	1 roasting chicken ($1\frac{1}{2}$ kg.)	1 roaster chicken ($3\frac{1}{2}$ lb.)
giblet stock ingredients (page 38)	giblet stock ingredients (page 38)	giblet stock ingredients (page 38)
2 oz. flour	50 g. flour	$\frac{1}{2}$ cup all-purpose flour
2 oz. lard	50 g. lard	$\frac{1}{4}$ cup lard
8 oz. mushrooms	225 g. mushrooms	2 cups mushrooms
1 medium onion, sliced	1 medium onion, sliced	1 medium onion, sliced
$\frac{1}{2}$ pint milk	3 dl. milk	$1\frac{1}{4}$ cups milk
4 teaspoons tomato purée	4 teaspoons tomato purée	4 teaspoons tomato paste
2–3 teaspoons strong paprika	2–3 teaspoons strong paprika	2–3 teaspoons strong paprika
2 teaspoons castor sugar	2 teaspoons castor sugar	2 teaspoons sugar
$\frac{1}{4}$ pint single or soured cream	$1\frac{1}{2}$ dl. single or soured cream	$\frac{2}{3}$ cup coffee or sour cream
salt and lemon juice	salt and lemon juice	salt and lemon juice
parsley sprigs for garnish	parsley sprigs for garnish	parsley sprigs for garnish

Joint and skin the chicken (pages 45 and 46). Clean the giblets and put with the carcass, skin and giblet stock ingredients into a saucepan. Simmer gently to make stock.

Flour the chicken joints and pat off any excess. Heat the lard in a sauté pan or flameproof casserole until it hazes and fry the chicken joints until golden brown all over. Meanwhile wash the mushrooms, reserve 4–5 for garnish, and quarter or halve the remainder, or leave whole if small. Remove the chicken from the pan and fry the mushrooms and onion until softened. Draw the pan from the heat and stir in 2–3 tablespoons flour, sufficient to absorb the fat. Gradually blend in the milk, bring to the boil and add $\frac{1}{2}$ pint (3 dl., $1\frac{1}{4}$ cups) strained giblet stock. Continue simmering and meanwhile mix together in a cup the tomato purée, paprika, sugar and cream. Blend in 2 tablespoons of the hot sauce and stir this mixture into the pan, seasoning to taste with salt and lemon juice. Replace the chicken joints in the sauce and, if necessary, add more stock so they are completely covered.

Put on the lid and simmer very gently on top of the stove or in a slow oven (300°F, 150°C, Gas Mark 2) for about 40 minutes or until the chicken legs are tender. Do not allow the sauce to boil as it may separate.

Serve in a border of fluffy boiled rice. Garnish the border with fried mushroom caps, paprika and parsley sprigs.

Serving suggestions:
a) Serve in a border of boiled and well-salted noodles, tossed with butter and a teaspoon grated lemon rind.
b) Serve with boiled new potatoes, tossed with butter and chopped fresh chives.

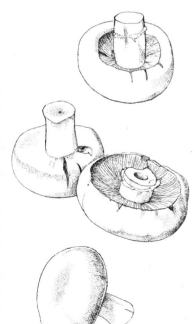

Chicken Marengo

Serves 4

This classic dish is reputed to have been invented by Napoleon's army chef to celebrate the victory at Marengo. He had to rely on the surrounding Italian countryside for its ingredients. He garnished it with eggs, deep fried in olive oil, and fresh water crayfish from local streams.

Imperial	Metric	American
1 roasting chicken	1 roasting chicken	1 roaster chicken
bay leaf, parsley and seasoning for stock	bay leaf, parsley and seasoning for stock	bay leaf, parsley and seasoning for stock
2 tablespoons olive oil	2 tablespoons olive oil	3 tablespoons olive oil
1–2 oz. butter	25–50 g. butter	2–4 tablespoons butter
flour for coating	flour for coating	flour for coating
2 medium onions, sliced	2 medium onions, sliced	2 medium onions, sliced
1 clove garlic, finely chopped	1 clove garlic, finely chopped	1 clove garlic, finely chopped
4–8 oz. mushrooms	100–225 g. mushrooms	1–2 cups mushrooms
4 fl. oz. dry white wine	1¼ dl. dry white wine	½ cup dry white wine
1 lb. ripe tomatoes or 1 (14 oz.) can tomatoes	½ kg. ripe tomatoes or 1 (400 g.) can tomatoes	1 lb. ripe tomatoes or 1 (14 oz.) can tomatoes
pinch each basil and marjoram	pinch each basil and marjoram	pinch each basil and marjoram
salt and fresh ground black pepper	salt and fresh ground black pepper	salt and fresh ground black pepper
lemon juice	lemon juice	lemon juice

Joint and skin the chicken (pages 45 and 46). Clean the giblets (page 38) and put with the carcass, herbs and seasoning in a saucepan with cold water to cover. Simmer to make stock.

Heat the oil and butter in a sauté pan or flameproof casserole. Flour the chicken joints, patting off surplus, and fry briskly until golden brown all over. Remove from the pan, add the onion, garlic and mushrooms and fry until the onions begin to turn colour. Add the wine and boil for 2–3 minutes. Add the skinned fresh or canned tomatoes coarsely chopped, herbs, chicken and sufficient giblet stock to cover the chicken. Bring to simmer, season to taste with salt, pepper and lemon juice. Cover and cook gently on a low flame or in a slow oven for about 40 minutes or until the legs are tender. Stir well and correct seasoning before serving with a bowl of rice or pasta.

Serving suggestions:
a) Arrange the chicken inside a rice border, garnished with langoustines (crayfish) tails fried in butter. Sprinkle the chicken with chopped fresh parsley and curls of lemon zest.
b) Arrange the chicken joints on a deep serving dish and garnish with triangles of fried bread topped with buttered spinach purée, flavoured with grated Parmesan cheese.

Swiss chicken with cheese and white wine sauce

Serves 4

This is a favourite way to prepare chicken in Switzerland and in the Alpine regions of France and Austria. It is an excellent dish for the cook/hostess as it can be prepared in advance and then finished in a hot oven when required.

Imperial	Metric	American
1 roasting chicken (2½–3 lb.)	1 roasting chicken (1¼–1½ kg.)	1 broiler-fryer chicken (2½–3 lb.)
onion, carrot and herbs for giblet stock	onion, carrot and herbs for giblet stock	onion, carrot and herbs for giblet stock
3 oz. butter	75 g. butter	6 tablespoons butter
1 tablespoon chopped fresh or dried tarragon leaves	1 tablespoon chopped fresh or dried tarragon leaves	1 tablespoon chopped fresh or dried tarragon leaves
salt and fresh ground black pepper	salt and fresh ground black pepper	salt and fresh ground black pepper
sauce:	*sauce:*	*sauce:*
2 oz. butter	50 g. butter	¼ cup butter
2 oz. flour	50 g. flour	½ cup all-purpose flour
¼ pint giblet stock	1½ dl. giblet stock	⅔ cup giblet stock
½ pint cream	3 dl. cream	1¼ cups cream
¼ pint dry white wine	1½ dl. dry white wine	⅔ cup dry white wine
2 oz. Gruyère or Emmenthal cheese, grated	50 g. Gruyère or Emmenthal cheese, grated	½ cup grated Gruyère or Emmenthal cheese
2 teaspoons French mustard	2 teaspoons French mustard	2 teaspoons French mustard
salt and black pepper	salt and black pepper	salt and black pepper
topping:	*topping:*	*topping:*
4 tablespoons toasted breadcrumbs	4 tablespoons toasted breadcrumbs	⅓ cup toasted bread crumbs
2 tablespoons grated cheese	2 tablespoons grated cheese	3 tablespoons grated cheese

Put the cleaned giblets in a pan with water, vegetables, herbs and seasoning to make stock.

Cream the butter and tarragon together and season with salt and freshly ground pepper. Spread this over the chicken and roast it in a preheated oven (400°F, 200°C, Gas Mark 6) for about 1 hour until tender. Turn the chicken from time to time and baste with the tarragon butter. Alternatively roast on a spit, basting frequently.

Meanwhile, make the sauce. Melt the butter. Draw from the heat and stir in the flour. Gradually blend in the giblet stock and then the cream. Return to the heat and bring to the simmer, stirring continuously. When it begins to bubble, add the wine and continue cooking very gently for 4–5 minutes. Stir in the cheese and mustard and season to taste. Cover and keep warm. When the chicken is cooked, carve it into four portions.

Butter a warmed gratin dish and pour a layer of sauce over the base. Arrange the chicken pieces on top and coat with the remaining sauce. Sprinkle with toasted crumbs and cheese and trickle over some of the tarragon butter from the roasting pan. The dish can now be set aside and finished off when required. For immediate use, put in the top of a preheated oven (425°F, 220°C, Gas Mark 7) and bake for 10–15 minutes until it has a bubbling golden crust. Alternatively the dish may be finished under the grill.

Serving suggestions:
Accompany with sauté potatoes or buttered noodles garnished with chopped fresh parsley, and a salad.

Paella a la Valenciana

Illustrated in colour opposite
Serves 6

There are various versions of Paella from the different regions of Spain, but the colourful Valencia dish is the most famous and makes a splendid party piece.

It should be cooked and served in the traditional paella pan, but a large skillet or frying pan does very well. In Spain the huge Mediterranean prawns called *gambas* are deep fried in oil in their shells and arranged on top of the Paella, but fresh or frozen large prawns or scampi may be used instead. When fresh mussels are not available, bottled ones may be substituted.

Imperial	Metric	American
1 roasting chicken	1 roasting chicken	1 roaster chicken
parsley, bay leaf and seasoning for stock	parsley, bay leaf and seasoning for stock	parsley, bay leaf and seasoning for stock
3 tablespoons olive oil	3 tablespoons olive oil	$\frac{1}{4}$ cup olive oil
1 large onion, sliced	1 large onion, sliced	1 large onion, sliced
1–2 cloves garlic, finely chopped	1–2 cloves garlic, finely chopped	1–2 cloves garlic, finely chopped
12 oz. rice	350 g. rice	$1\frac{3}{4}$ cups rice
1 large or 2 small red or green peppers	1 large or 2 small red or green peppers	1 large or 2 small red or green sweet peppers
1 quart fresh mussels	generous 1 litre fresh mussels	5 cups fresh mussels
4 fl. oz. dry white wine	$1\frac{1}{4}$ dl. dry white wine	$\frac{1}{2}$ cup dry white wine
good pinch powdered saffron	good pinch powdered saffron	good pinch powdered saffron
6 oz. Chorizo or garlic sausage	175 g. Chorizo or garlic sausage	$\frac{1}{3}$ lb. Chorizo or garlic sausage
2–3 tablespoons cooked green peas (optional)	2–3 tablespoons cooked green peas (optional)	3–4 tablespoons cooked green peas (optional)
12 large prawns or scampi	12 large prawns or scampi	12 Dublin prawns or jumbo shrimp
lemon wedges for garnish	lemon wedges for garnish	lemon wedges for garnish

Divide chicken into 6 joints and skin (pages 45 and 46). Put carcass, skin and cleaned giblets into a saucepan of cold water with herbs, seasoning and make a well-flavoured stock.

Heat the oil in a paella or frying pan and fry the chicken joints until golden all over. Remove and fry the onion and garlic until softened, without colouring. Add the rice and continue frying until a pale biscuit colour, stirring continuously. Put in the chicken and strain in sufficient stock to cover. Simmer over low heat, adding more stock as it is absorbed and stirring frequently. Slice the peppers thinly, after removing seeds and membrane, add to pan. Clean and beard the mussels (page 78) discarding any that are damaged or float. Put into a saucepan with the wine, cover and cook for 10–15 minutes until the shells open. Lift out the mussels and keep them warm in a folded cloth. Strain the liquor into the rice, add saffron and stir well. Continue simmering until the rice is just tender and the stock absorbed.

Meanwhile, fry sliced or chopped Chorizo and add to the rice with the cooked peas. Add the prepared prawns or scampi; these will toughen if overcooked. Remove the top shells of the mussels and arrange the bottom halves containing the mussels on top of the rice. Garnish with lemon wedges. Serve with a tossed green salad.

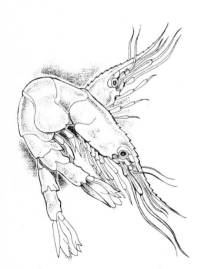

Sauces for the bird

White sauces (Béchamel grasse)
Ordinary white sauce is made with milk added to a roux base of equal quantities of butter and flour, but if the liquid used is half chicken or giblet stock and half milk, a richer more flavoursome sauce results, which is called Béchamel grasse. It can be used in a number of ways.

Basic Béchamel sauce

for coating hot poultry, game or vegetables

Imperial	Metric	American
2 oz. butter	50 g. butter	$\frac{1}{4}$ cup butter
2 oz. flour	50 g. flour	$\frac{1}{2}$ cup all-purpose flour
$\frac{1}{4}$ pint milk	$1\frac{1}{2}$ dl. milk	$\frac{2}{3}$ cup milk
$\frac{1}{4}$ pint good chicken stock (page 38)	$1\frac{1}{2}$ dl. good chicken stock (page 38)	$\frac{2}{3}$ cup good chicken stock (page 38)
pinch nutmeg or mace	pinch nutmeg or mace	pinch nutmeg or mace
salt and ground white pepper	salt and ground white pepper	salt and ground white pepper

Melt the butter. Draw the pan from the heat and stir in the flour to make a smooth roux. Gradually blend in the milk and then the strained stock. Return to the heat and bring to the boil, beating and stirring continuously to prevent lumps forming as the sauce thickens. Add the nutmeg and season well with salt and pepper. Cook very gently for 5 minutes or longer, stirring frequently. If the flour is not sufficiently cooked the sauce will taste floury. The finished sauce should cling to the back of a wooden spoon and coat it evenly.

If properly stirred the sauce will be smooth, but should there be any lumps, they can easily be dispersed with a rotary whisk. Cover to prevent a skin forming and stand the saucepan in a *bain marie* (a pan of hot water) if it is to be kept warm. Stir before using.

Lemon Béchamel sauce
Sharpen the cooked Béchamel with 2–3 tablespoons fresh lemon juice.

Parsley Béchamel sauce
Add 2–3 tablespoons chopped parsley to the cooked Béchamel.

Cheese Béchamel sauce
When the Béchamel is cooked, draw the pan from the heat and stir in 3–4 oz. (75–100 g.) grated hard cheese. Stir until melted, but do not boil as the cheese will go stringy.

Egg Béchamel sauce
Add 2 chopped hard-boiled eggs to Parsley or Cheese Béchamel.

Velouté sauce
Beat 2 egg yolks into 3 tablespoons (U.S. scant $\frac{1}{4}$ cup) cream. Blend in 3 tablespoons Béchamel and stir this mixture back into the sauce. Sharpen to taste with lemon juice and cook, stirring, until slightly thickened.

Conical sieve for liquids (chinois)

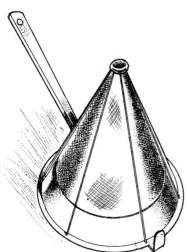

Blanquette sauce

for boiled bird and
vols-au-vent

Imperial	Metric	American
1 medium onion, thinly sliced	1 medium onion, thinly sliced	1 medium onion, thinly sliced
2 rashers bacon	2 rashers bacon	2 bacon slices
4 oz. mushrooms, sliced	100 g. mushrooms, sliced	1 cup sliced mushrooms
1 stick celery, finely chopped	1 stick celery, finely chopped	1 stalk celery, finely chopped
2 oz. butter	50 g. butter	$\frac{1}{4}$ cup butter
2–3 tablespoons flour	2–3 tablespoons flour	3–4 tablespoons flour
$\frac{1}{2}$ pint milk	3 dl. milk	$1\frac{1}{4}$ cups milk
$\frac{1}{2}$ pint good chicken stock (page 38)	3 dl. good chicken stock (page 38)	$1\frac{1}{4}$ cups good chicken stock (page 38)
pinch nutmeg or mace	pinch nutmeg or mace	pinch nutmeg or mace
salt, pepper and lemon juice	salt, pepper and lemon juice	salt, pepper and lemon juice

Fry the onion, bacon, mushrooms and celery slowly in the butter until softened, but not coloured. Draw the pan from the heat and stir in sufficient flour to absorb the fat and make a smooth roux. Gradually blend in the milk and the strained chicken stock. Bring to the simmer and flavour with nutmeg. Season to taste and sharpen with a little lemon juice. Cook gently for 10–15 minutes, stirring frequently.

French onion sauce
Make as Blanquette sauce, using 2 chopped medium onions and omitting bacon, mushrooms and celery.

Panada

This is a thick binding sauce for soufflés, mousses and croquettes. Make as Basic Béchamel, but twice as thick by omitting milk and using only the $\frac{1}{4}$ pint ($1\frac{1}{2}$ dl., $\frac{2}{3}$ cup) chicken stock.

Bread sauce

for roasted and
grilled bird

Imperial	Metric	American
1 medium onion	1 medium onion	1 medium onion
6–8 whole cloves	6–8 whole cloves	6–8 whole cloves
about $\frac{1}{2}$ pint milk	about 3 dl. milk	about $1\frac{1}{4}$ cups milk
1 bay leaf	1 bay leaf	1 bay leaf
4–6 slices white bread	4–6 slices white bread	4–6 slices white bread
$\frac{1}{2}$ oz. butter	15 g. butter	1 tablespoon butter
pinch nutmeg or mace	pinch nutmeg or mace	pinch nutmeg or mace
salt and freshly ground pepper	salt and freshly ground pepper	salt and freshly ground pepper
2–3 tablespoons cream	2–3 tablespoons cream	3–4 tablespoons cream

Peel the onion and spike the bottom with the cloves. Put into a small pan, cloves downwards, and add the milk and bay leaf. Heat very slowly to infuse the flavours. Meanwhile, cut the crusts off the bread and dice the slices. When the milk boils, draw the pan off the heat. Add the bread and leave in a warm place for 30 minutes or longer. Do not boil or the bread will become rubbery.

Remove the onion and bay leaf. Add the butter, nutmeg and season well with salt and pepper. Whisk until creamy. If too thick, add a little more milk. Stir in the cream before serving.

Barbecue sauce

for marinating and
basting during
spit roasting and
grilling

Illustrated in colour on the jacket

Imperial	Metric	American
1 medium onion, chopped	1 medium onion, chopped	1 medium onion, chopped
1 tablespoon vegetable oil	1 tablespoon vegetable oil	1 tablespoon vegetable oil
1 (14 oz.) can peeled tomatoes	1 (400 g.) can peeled tomatoes	1 (14 oz.) can peeled tomatoes
3 sticks celery, finely chopped	3 sticks celery, finely chopped	3 stalks celery, finely chopped
3 tablespoons tarragon vinegar	3 tablespoons tarragon vinegar	scant $\frac{1}{4}$ cup tarragon vinegar
3 tablespoons tomato ketchup	3 tablespoons tomato ketchup	scant $\frac{1}{4}$ cup tomato catsup
1 tablespoon Worcestershire sauce	1 tablespoon Worcestershire sauce	1 tablespoon Worcestershire sauce
1 clove garlic, crushed	1 clove garlic, crushed	1 clove garlic, crushed
3 bay leaves	3 bay leaves	3 bay leaves
$\frac{1}{2}$ lemon, thinly sliced	$\frac{1}{2}$ lemon, thinly sliced	$\frac{1}{2}$ lemon, thinly sliced
$\frac{1}{2}$ pint chicken stock	3 dl. chicken stock	$1\frac{1}{4}$ cups chicken stock
salt and pepper	salt and pepper	salt and pepper

Fry the onion slowly in the hot oil until just turning colour. Add the other ingredients and simmer for 20–30 minutes. Remove the bay leaves and lemon slices before using and adjust the seasoning.

Apricot and honey barbecue sauce

This sauce is an attractive alternative for a spitted chicken and is ideal for an indoor barbecue dish, when the chicken is jointed and baked in the oven.

Imperial	Metric	American
1 (15 oz.) can apricot halves	1 (425 g.) can apricot halves	1 (15 oz.) can apricot halves
4 teaspoons soy sauce	4 teaspoons soy sauce	4 teaspoons soy sauce
4 teaspoons honey	4 teaspoons honey	4 teaspoons honey
4 teaspoons tomato ketchup	4 teaspoons tomato ketchup	4 teaspoons tomato catsup
$\frac{1}{4}$ teaspoon rosemary	$\frac{1}{4}$ teaspoon rosemary	$\frac{1}{4}$ teaspoon rosemary
4 teaspoons lemon juice	4 teaspoons lemon juice	4 teaspoons lemon juice
$\frac{1}{2}$ pint stock (page 38)	3 dl. stock (page 38)	$1\frac{1}{4}$ cups stock (page 38)
seasoning	seasoning	seasoning
1 chicken, jointed	1 chicken, jointed	1 chicken, cut up
oil	oil	oil

Strain off the apricot juice and put the fruit into a blender or sieve, reserving 4 apricot halves for garnish. Heat the purée gently in a saucepan with the soy sauce, honey, tomato ketchup and rosemary, until the honey is melted. Sharpen with lemon juice.

Heat the oven to 425°F, 220°C, Gas Mark 7. Place the chicken joints in an oiled roasting pan and brush with oil. Pour over the sauce and bake for 10 minutes, then turn, baste with the sauce and brown on the other side. Reduce the heat (375°F, 190°C, Gas Mark 5) and continue cooking for a further 20–25 minutes or until the chicken is tender, basting occasionally.

Remove the chicken to a warm serving dish. Add the stock to the roasting pan and boil up, scraping up the residue from the bottom of the pan. Reduce slightly, adjust the seasoning and pour over the chicken joints. Garnish with the remaining apricot halves.

Barbecued chicken (page 11)

Bercy sauce

for boiled or roast bird and hot chicken mousse

Makes ½ pint (3 dl., 1¼ cups)

Imperial	Metric	American
1 small onion	1 small onion	1 small onion
2 oz. butter	50 g. butter	¼ cup butter
4 fl. oz. white wine or cider	1¼ dl. white wine or cider	½ cup white wine or cider
8 fl. oz. chicken stock (page 38)	2½ dl. chicken stock (page 38)	1 cup chicken stock (page 38)
1 tablespoon flour	1 tablespoon flour	1 tablespoon flour
4 fl. oz. cream	1¼ dl. cream	½ cup cream
2 teaspoons chopped parsley	2 teaspoons chopped parsley	2 teaspoons chopped parsley
salt and pepper	salt and pepper	salt and pepper
lemon juice to taste	lemon juice to taste	lemon juice to taste

Fry the finely chopped onion in half the butter over a low heat, until softened. Add the wine and chicken stock and boil, uncovered, until reduced by half.

Make *beurre manié* (kneaded butter) by creaming together the remaining butter with the flour. Form the mixture into marble-sized balls. Drop these one at a time into the sauce, stirring until it thickens. When it is of coating consistency, blend about 5 tablespoons of the sauce into the cream and stir this mixture into the sauce. Add the parsley. Season.

White devil sauce

for marinating and basting

For 4 chicken breasts

Imperial	Metric	American
¼ pint double cream	1½ dl. double cream	⅔ cup whipping cream
2 tablespoons lemon juice	2 tablespoons lemon juice	3 tablespoons lemon juice
2 tablespoons mango chutney	2 tablespoons mango chutney	3 tablespoons mango chutney
1 tablespoon mushroom ketchup	1 tablespoon mushroom ketchup	1 tablespoon mushroom catsup
2–3 teaspoons Dijon mustard	2–3 teaspoons Dijon mustard	2–3 teaspoons Dijon mustard
2 tablespoons soy sauce	2 tablespoons soy sauce	3 tablespoons soy sauce
dash Tabasco sauce	dash Tabasco sauce	dash Tabasco sauce

Thicken the cream by stirring in the lemon juice. Then add the other ingredients and mix well.

Dark devil sauce

for marinating and basting

For 4 chicken legs

Imperial	Metric	American
4 tablespoons tomato ketchup	4 tablespoons tomato ketchup	⅓ cup tomato catsup
2 tablespoons olive oil	2 tablespoons olive oil	3 tablespoons olive oil
2 tablespoons brown pickle sauce	2 tablespoons brown pickle sauce	3 tablespoons brown pickle sauce
1 tablespoon cranberry or redcurrant jelly	1 tablespoon cranberry or redcurrant jelly	1 tablespoon cranberry or red currant jelly
1 tablespoon tarragon vinegar	1 tablespoon tarragon vinegar	1 tablespoon tarragon vinegar
1 tablespoon Worcestershire sauce	1 tablespoon Worcestershire sauce	1 tablespoon Worcestershire sauce
grated rind and juice 1 orange	grated rind and juice 1 orange	grated rind and juice 1 orange
salt and freshly ground black pepper	salt and freshly ground black pepper	salt and freshly ground black pepper

Mix all the ingredients together, seasoning to taste.

Soured cream and garlic marinade

This is particularly good for frozen chicken. The thawed joints should be covered in the marinade and left for several hours or overnight in the refrigerator. Thick cream may be soured with extra lemon juice or yoghurt used instead.

Imperial	Metric	American
$\frac{1}{4}$ pint soured cream	$1\frac{1}{2}$ dl. soured cream	$\frac{2}{3}$ cup sour cream
1 large clove garlic, crushed	1 large clove garlic, crushed	1 large clove garlic, crushed
1 tablespoon lemon juice	1 tablespoon lemon juice	1 tablespoon lemon juice
1 teaspoon dried thyme or rosemary	1 teaspoon dried thyme or rosemary	1 teaspoon dried thyme or rosemary
1 teaspoon celery salt	1 teaspoon celery salt	1 teaspoon celery salt
$\frac{1}{2}$ teaspoon pepper	$\frac{1}{2}$ teaspoon pepper	$\frac{1}{2}$ teaspoon pepper
$\frac{1}{2}$ teaspoon paprika	$\frac{1}{2}$ teaspoon paprika	$\frac{1}{2}$ teaspoon paprika
$\frac{1}{2}$ teaspoon salt	$\frac{1}{2}$ teaspoon salt	$\frac{1}{2}$ teaspoon salt

Combine all the ingredients and use for marinating and basting, during spit-roasting or grilling.

Thick mayonnaise

Makes $\frac{1}{4}$ pint ($1\frac{1}{2}$ dl., $\frac{2}{3}$ cup)

Imperial	Metric	American
2 egg yolks	2 egg yolks	2 egg yolks
$\frac{1}{4}$ pint olive oil	$1\frac{1}{2}$ dl. olive oil	$\frac{2}{3}$ cup olive oil
$\frac{1}{4}$ teaspoon salt	$\frac{1}{4}$ teaspoon salt	$\frac{1}{4}$ teaspoon salt
freshly ground pepper	freshly ground pepper	freshly ground pepper
$\frac{1}{4}$ teaspoon French mustard (optional)	$\frac{1}{4}$ teaspoon French mustard (optional)	$\frac{1}{4}$ teaspoon French mustard (optional)
2 teaspoons lemon juice or tarragon vinegar	2 teaspoons lemon juice or tarragon vinegar	2 teaspoons lemon juice or tarragon vinegar

Put the egg yolks into a basin, wrapped in a cloth to prevent it slipping on the table. Stir with a wooden spoon until creamy. Trickle in the oil, a few drops at a time, stirring steadily in the same direction and at an even speed until the sauce is quite stiff, when the oil can be added a little faster. Adjust the seasoning and sharpen to taste with lemon juice or tarragon vinegar.

Tunny fish mayonnaise
Pound or sieve 1 ($2\frac{1}{2}$ oz., 65 g.) can tunny fish with its oil. Add to $\frac{1}{4}$ pint ($1\frac{1}{2}$ dl., $\frac{2}{3}$ cup) thick mayonnaise made without mustard. Mix well and sharpen with lemon juice.

Tartare sauce *for grilled or cold bird*
Make $\frac{1}{4}$ pint ($1\frac{1}{2}$ dl., $\frac{2}{3}$ cup) thick mayonnaise, omitting the vinegar. Stir in 2 teaspoons each of finely chopped capers, gherkins, shallots or cocktail onions and 1 tablespoon chopped fresh parsley. Season to taste with mustard and lemon juice.

Gribiche sauce *for cold bird and chicken salad*
Add the sieved yolks of 2 hard-boiled eggs to the raw yolks when making $\frac{1}{4}$ pint ($1\frac{1}{2}$ dl., $\frac{2}{3}$ cup) thick mayonnaise. When the mayonnaise has thickened, stir in the chopped whites of the hard-boiled eggs, 4 teaspoons finely chopped gherkins and 4 teaspoons chopped fresh parsley. Season well and sharpen with tarragon vinegar.

Starters
and savouries

Petites royales au Parmesan

Serves 6

A *royale* is a savoury custard and these are particularly good made with a strong chicken stock (page 38) or the giblet stock from roast turkey. When they are set, they are covered with cream and grated cheese and toasted until golden brown on top. These savoury custards can be served as a starter or a savoury.

Imperial	Metric	American
2 whole eggs and 3 yolks	2 whole eggs and 3 yolks	2 whole eggs and 3 yolks
$\frac{1}{4}$ pint double cream	$1\frac{1}{2}$ dl. double cream	$\frac{2}{3}$ cup heavy cream
$\frac{3}{4}$ pint strong chicken or turkey stock	scant $\frac{1}{2}$ litre strong chicken or turkey stock	2 cups strong chicken or turkey stock
1 teaspoon each chopped parsley, chives and tarragon	1 teaspoon each chopped parsley, chives and tarragon	1 teaspoon each chopped parsley, chives and tarragon
salt and pepper	salt and pepper	salt and pepper
1 oz. Parmesan cheese, grated	25 g. Parmesan cheese, grated	$\frac{1}{4}$ cup grated Parmesan cheese
2 oz. Gruyère or other hard cheese, grated	50 g. Gruyère or other hard cheese, grated	$\frac{1}{2}$ cup grated Gruyère or other hard cheese

Beat the eggs well together with 2 tablespoons cream. Heat the stock slowly with the herbs. When it comes to the boil, strain it on to the eggs, stirring vigorously. Season. Butter 6 dariole moulds, or small moulds, $\frac{1}{4}$ pint ($1\frac{1}{2}$ dl., $\frac{2}{3}$ cup) size, and fill with the custard.

Put the darioles into a stewpan with about 1 inch ($2\frac{1}{2}$ cm.) water in the bottom and simmer gently on top of the stove, or in a bain marie in a moderate oven (325°F, 170°C, Gas Mark 3) for 1 hour or until set. Chill thoroughly.

Butter a fireproof serving dish or individual shallow bowls. Turn out the royales, pour over the remaining cream. Mix the grated cheeses together and sprinkle generously over the royales. Place in the top of a hot oven (425°F, 220°C, Gas Mark 7) or under the grill, until the crust is golden and bubbling. Serve immediately with thin brown bread sandwiches of cress or cucumber.

Pâté de campagne

This French country style pâté can be made with chicken, guinea fowl or pheasant, or a mixture.* The birds can either be part-roasted or boiled according to age and convenience, until the flesh can be removed and chopped roughly or put through a coarse mincer. If using an electric mincer be careful to run it only for a few seconds at a time or the traditional rough texture of the pâté will be lost.

Imperial	Metric	American
4 oz. streaky bacon rashers	100 g. streaky bacon rashers	¼ lb. bacon slices
2 fresh bay leaves	2 fresh bay leaves	2 fresh bay leaves
1 lb. chicken or pheasant meat*	450 g. chicken or pheasant meat*	1 lb. chicken or pheasant meat*
4 oz. pickled belly pork	100 g. pickled belly pork	¼ lb. salt pork
1 clove garlic, crushed	1 clove garlic, crushed	1 clove garlic, crushed
2 tablespoons chopped fresh parsley	2 tablespoons chopped fresh parsley	3 tablespoons chopped fresh parsley
pinch dried thyme	pinch dried thyme	pinch dried thyme
pinch crushed dried rosemary	pinch crushed dried rosemary	pinch crushed dried rosemary
salt and freshly ground black pepper	salt and freshly ground black pepper	salt and freshly ground black pepper
1 egg, beaten	1 egg, beaten	1 egg, beaten
3 tablespoons double cream	3 tablespoons double cream	scant ¼ cup whipping cream
3–4 oz. chicken or game livers	75–100 g. chicken or game livers	about ¼ lb. chicken or game livers
1½ oz. butter	40 g. butter	3 tablespoons butter
2 tablespoons brandy	2 tablespoons brandy	3 tablespoons brandy
lemon juice to taste	lemon juice to taste	lemon juice to taste

Remove the rind from the bacon rashers. Lay a bay leaf in the bottom of a pint-sized terrine or casserole dish and place one end of the rashers on top of it, radiating out in a star design with the other ends hanging outside the dish.

Chop and mince the chicken or game meat roughly with the pickled pork. Add the garlic and herbs and season well. Stir in the egg and cream. Divide the chicken or game livers into neat pieces, removing any stained pieces, and sauté quickly in the hot butter until just firm. Pour the surplus butter into the pâté mixture. Warm the brandy in a little pan or soup ladle, set alight and pour flaming over the livers, shake until the flames die out. Set the liver aside and scrape the juices from the pan into the pâté mixture. Sharpen to taste with the lemon juice and adjust the seasoning.

Half fill the bacon-lined terrine with the pâté mixture and press down. Cover with sautéed livers. Cover with remaining minced mixture and fold over the bacon rashers. Place a bay leaf on top. Put on the buttered lid and stand the terrine in a roasting pan with ½ inch (2 cm.) water in the bottom. Bake in a preheated oven (325°F, 170°C, Gas Mark 3) for 1½ hours or until set.

Allow to chill overnight before cutting, or it will crumble. It can be served in the terrine or turned out.

In France, *terrine* is served with crusty bread and fresh butter, in England it is usually accompanied with hot toast wrapped in a napkin.

Chicken and almond dip

Makes 1 pint (6 dl., 2½ cups)

This can be served as a cocktail savoury or as a first course for lunch or dinner.

Imperial	Metric	American
6 oz. cooked chicken, minced	175 g. cooked chicken, minced	¾ cup ground cooked chicken
4 oz. button mushrooms, minced	100 g. button mushrooms, minced	1 cup ground button mushrooms
2 tablespoons ground almonds	2 tablespoons ground almonds	3 tablespoons ground almonds
4 tablespoons thick mayonnaise (page 65)	4 tablespoons thick mayonnaise (page 65)	⅓ cup thick mayonnaise (page 65)
4 tablespoons soured cream	4 tablespoons soured cream	⅓ cup sour cream
salt and freshly ground black pepper	salt and freshly ground black pepper	salt and freshly ground black pepper
snipped chives and paprika for garnish	snipped chives and paprika for garnish	snipped chives and paprika for garnish

Mix the dip ingredients together and season to taste.

For cocktails, turn the dip into a large bowl, garnish and surround with prepared vegetable and biscuit dippers.

For a starter, spoon the dip into individual ramekin dishes and garnish. Place each ramekin on a small plate and surround with prepared vegetable and biscuit dippers.

Dippers
a) Raw cauliflower florets on cocktail sticks.
b) Tiny button mushrooms on cocktail sticks.
c) Small sticks of celery head with leaves.
d) Sticks of raw young carrot, cut with a crinkle chipper.
e) Small cocktail biscuits or crackers.

Tagliatelli Tetrazzini

Serves 4

This rich pasta dish was named after the famous opera singer, Tetrazzini, who loved good food. It can be made with the flat noodles called tagliatelli or with macaroni. Serve in individual ramekins for a first course, or bake in a gratin dish and serve as a lunch or supper dish, with tossed green salad.

Imperial	Metric	American
8 oz. tagliatelli or macaroni	225 g. tagliatelli or macaroni	½ lb. tagliatelli or macaroni
1 quart water	generous 1 litre water	5 cups water
2 teaspoons salt	2 teaspoons salt	2 teaspoons salt
8 oz. mushrooms, sliced	225 g. mushrooms, sliced	2 cups sliced mushrooms
1 oz. butter	25 g. butter	2 tablespoons butter
½ pint Béchamel sauce (page 60)	3 dl. Béchamel sauce (page 60)	1¼ cups Béchamel sauce (page 60)
6 fl. oz. double cream	2 dl. double cream	¾ cup whipping cream
2 tablespoons sherry seasoning	2 tablespoons sherry seasoning	3 tablespoons sherry seasoning
8 oz. cooked chicken	225 g. cooked chicken	½ lb. cooked chicken
grated Parmesan cheese	grated Parmesan cheese	grated Parmesan cheese
2 tablespoons flaked almonds	2 tablespoons flaked almonds	3 tablespoons flaked almonds

Cook the tagliatelli in the boiling, salted water for 15 minutes or until just tender and drain in a colander. Meanwhile, fry the mushrooms in the hot butter for 3–5 minutes in a large sauté pan, stirring well. Mix in the drained pasta. Heat the béchamel sauce gently, gradually stirring in the cream. When hot, but not boiling, stir in the sherry and adjust the seasoning. Stir half the sauce into the pasta and mushroom mixture. Add the chopped chicken to the remaining sauce.

Turn the pasta mixture into a gratin dish or individual ramekins, hollow out the centre and fill with the chicken mixture. Sprinkle the pasta border with grated Parmesan cheese and the chicken mixture with flaked almonds. Brown in the top of a hot oven (425°F, 220°C, Gas Mark 7) or under the grill.

Chicken and pasta salad

Serves 4

Pasta is made in a variety of shapes which makes an attractive base for salads. You can use shells, farfalle (butterflies) or even elbow macaroni. The salads can be served in small portions for a starter or in larger portions for a supper dish.

Imperial	Metric	American
6 oz. pasta shells or farfalle	175 g. pasta shells or farfalle	6 oz. pasta shells or farfalle
3 pints water	1½ litres water	7½ cups water
2 teaspoons salt	2 teaspoons salt	2 teaspoons salt
3–4 tablespoons French dressing	3–4 tablespoons French dressing	4–5 tablespoons French dressing
1 tablespoon chopped fresh parsley	1 tablespoon chopped fresh parsley	1 tablespoon chopped fresh parsley
1 tablespoon finely chopped chives or spring onions	1 tablespoon finely chopped chives or spring onions	1 tablespoon finely chopped chives or scallions
8 oz. cooked chicken meat	225 g. cooked chicken meat	½ lb. cooked chicken meat
2 oz. cooked tongue, diced	50 g. cooked tongue, diced	½ cup diced cooked tongue
2 oz. cooked ham, diced	50 g. cooked ham, diced	½ cup diced cooked ham
2 tablespoons chopped celery heart	2 tablespoons chopped celery heart	3 tablespoons chopped celery heart
2 tablespoons chopped pimentos	2 tablespoons chopped pimentos	3 tablespoons chopped pimentos
4–5 tablespoons Gribiche sauce (page 65)	4–5 tablespoons Gribiche sauce (page 65)	5–6 tablespoons Gribiche sauce (page 65)
celery leaves for garnish	celery leaves for garnish	celery leaves for garnish

Drop the pasta shells into the boiling water with the salt added and cook briskly for about 12 minutes until just tender. Drain well in a colander. Mix with sufficient French dressing to moisten well and add the parsley and chives. Leave to cool. Cut up the chicken and combine with the tongue, ham, celery and pimento. Mix in the Gribiche sauce.

Pile in the centre of a serving dish and surround with pasta shells. Garnish with tufts of celery leaves.

Supper dishes and snacks

Chicken risotto Milanaise

Serves 4

Risotto or savoury rice is an ideal way to use the stock, giblets and carcass meat left from a bird which has been jointed for casseroling.

Imperial	Metric	American
1–2 onions, sliced	1–2 onions, sliced	1–2 onions, sliced
2 tablespoons olive oil	2 tablespoons olive oil	3 tablespoons olive oil
8 oz. rice	225 g. rice	generous 1 cup rice
about 1½ pints chicken stock	about 1 litre chicken stock	about 3¾ cups chicken stock
4 oz. button mushrooms	100 g. button mushrooms	1 cup button mushrooms
chicken giblets and carcass meat	chicken giblets and carcass meat	chicken giblets and carcass meat
pinch powdered saffron	pinch powdered saffron	pinch powdered saffron
3–4 oz. cheese, grated	75–100 g. cheese, grated	¾–1 cup grated cheese
paprika and salt to taste	paprika and salt to taste	paprika and salt to taste
1–2 roasted peppers for garnish	1–2 roasted peppers for garnish	1–2 roasted sweet peppers for garnish

Fry the sliced onion gently in the hot oil until softened. Stir in the rice (unwashed) and continue frying, stirring continuously until just turning colour. Add sufficient stock to float the rice. Cover and simmer over a low heat until the liquid is absorbed. Add the sliced mushrooms. Continue adding stock as it is absorbed, stirring frequently until the rice is just tender—about 35 minutes. Meanwhile chop coarsely and add the cooked liver, heart and gizzard and the meat stripped from the carcass. Stir in just enough saffron to flavour the rice and colour it a delicate yellow. Draw the pan from the heat, stir in the grated cheese and season with paprika and salt.

Cut the peppers in wedges and remove pips and membrane. Brush with oil and roast on both sides under the grill.

Pile the rice in a warm serving bowl and garnish with roasted peppers. Serve with a tossed green salad.

Crochette Milanaise

Serves 4

These savoury patties are a favourite way to use up surplus risotto, for a first course or supper dish.

Imperial	Metric	American
1 large or 2 small eggs	1 large or 2 small eggs	1 large or 2 small eggs
about 10 oz. cooked risotto	about 275 g. cooked risotto	2 cups cooked risotto
breadcrumbs	breadcrumbs	bread crumbs
oil or butter	oil or butter	oil or butter

Mix the egg well into the risotto, which should remain a stiff mixture. Take a tablespoon at a time and shape with floured fingers into a pattie. Coat with crumbs, pressing them well in, and fry in shallow hot oil or butter until golden, turning once.

Drain on absorbent paper and serve with watercress tossed in French dressing for a first course, or with buttered spinach for a supper dish.

Stuffed peppers
Risotto also makes an excellent stuffing for red or green peppers, which are baked and served with tomato sauce as a starter, or lunch or supper dish.

Toasted sandwiches

These are hearty savoury snacks for lunch or a fireside supper.

Triple-decker club sandwich

For each sandwich:
Toast 3 slices of bread, remove the crusts and spread with softened butter.
Bottom layer: Cover with sliced chicken, spread with mayonnaise and top with sliced cucumber.
Second layer: Cover with sliced tomato, season well, top with crisply grilled bacon rashers and garnish with leaves of lettuce heart.
Top layer: Press on firmly and secure with 4 cocktail sticks or toothpicks, each topped with a stuffed olive.
Quarter the sandwich when serving.

Toasted double-decker sandwich

For each sandwich:
Toast 2 slices of bread, remove the crusts and spread with softened butter.

Filling 1:
Bottom layer: Cover with sliced cold chicken and cooked ham. Spread with sweet pickle and top with watercress sprigs.
Top layer: Cover with crumbled Roquefort or Danish blue cheese and grill until the cheese melts. Place on top of the sandwich.

Filling 2:
Bottom layer: Mix chopped cooked chicken with well seasoned cream cheese. Spread on toast, sprinkle with chopped salted peanuts and top with garden cress.
Top layer: Cover with sliced tomatoes, season with salt and pepper and sugar and grill until just colouring. Place on top of sandwich and garnish with cress.

Filling 3:
Bottom layer: Cover with sliced cooked chicken, spread with mango or apricot chutney.
Top layer: Top with crumbled Cheshire cheese and grill until the cheese melts. Place on top of the sandwich and garnish with parsley.

Fried sandwiches

Remove the crusts from the bread slices and spread with softened butter. Cover the bottom slice with the chosen filling, press the top slice firmly on top and cut into fingers. Shallow fry in hot butter or lard until crisp and golden, turning once. Drain on soft paper and serve immediately.
Filling 1: Sliced cooked chicken, spread with sweet pickle and top with sliced Bel Paese or Gouda cheese.
Filling 2: Chopped cooked chicken and diced ham bound with thick cold Cheese béchamel sauce (page 60).

Cheesy chicken à la King

Measure with a tea cup for 4 servings, with a larger breakfast cup for 6 servings

Imperial	Metric	American
1½ cups Cheese béchamel sauce (page 60)	1½ cups Cheese béchamel sauce (page 60)	1½ cups Cheese béchamel sauce (page 60)
1½ cups diced cooked chicken	1½ cups diced cooked chicken	1½ cups diced cooked chicken
½ cup chopped canned pimentos	½ cup chopped canned pimentos	½ cup chopped canned pimientos
½ cup canned button mushrooms	½ cup canned button mushrooms	½ cup canned button mushrooms
1 egg yolk	1 egg yolk	1 egg yolk
1 tablespoon sherry	1 tablespoon sherry	1 tablespoon sherry
salt and pepper	salt and pepper	salt and pepper
slices of wholemeal or white bread	slices of wholemeal or white bread	slices of wholewheat or white bread
3–4 tablespoons flaked almonds	3–4 tablespoons flaked almonds	4–5 tablespoons flaked almonds

Warm the cheese bechamel sauce over a gentle heat, stirring continuously. Mix in the chicken and pimento. Halve the mushrooms and add. Mix 2 spoonfuls of the sauce with the beaten egg yolk, then stir into the pan. Heat the sauce until thickened, but do not boil. Flavour with sherry and season to taste.

Toast one slice of bread for each serving. Remove the crusts, cover with the chicken mixture and sprinkle with flaked almonds which have been toasted under the grill until crisp and golden.

Cheesy chicken à la King makes a tasty filling for vol-au-vent cases and Savoury pancakes (see next recipe).

Savoury pancakes

One filled pancake per person is sufficient for a first course; two make a tasty supper dish served with green peas or salad.

Make 8 thin pancakes in a 7–8-inch (18–20-cm.) frying pan. Spoon 2–3 tablespoons of hot Cheesy chicken à la King filling down the centre of each pancake and fold over the two sides on top of it. Place the filled pancakes in a buttered gratin dish, brush well with melted butter and sprinkle generously with grated cheese. Place in a pre-heated oven (400°F, 200°C, Gas Mark 6) for about 15 minutes, to heat through and crisp on top.

Blanquette of chicken (page 43), using boned chicken meat, is also a good filling for pancakes.

1. Spoon filling down centre of pancake

2. Fold over sides on top of filling

3. Sprinkle with grated cheese

Chicken and cream cheese kromeskies

Makes 8

These little savoury puffs are fried crisp and golden. They are served hot, either as a starter or cocktail or dinner savoury, or with tomato sauce as a supper dish.

Imperial	Metric	American
4 oz. cooked chicken meat	100 g. cooked chicken meat	$\frac{1}{4}$ lb. cooked chicken meat
3 oz. cream cheese	75 g. cream cheese	6 tablespoons cream cheese
2 teaspoons finely chopped onion	2 teaspoons finely chopped onion	2 teaspoons finely chopped onion
2 teaspoons grated Parmesan cheese	2 teaspoons grated Parmesan cheese	2 teaspoons grated Parmesan cheese
salt and paprika pepper	salt and paprika pepper	salt and paprika pepper
4 oz. shortcrust pastry (page 25) (using 4 oz. flour etc.)	100 g. shortcrust pastry (page 25) (using 100 g. flour etc.)	$\frac{1}{4}$ lb. shortcrust pastry (page 25) (using 1 cup all-purpose flour etc.)
deep fat for frying	deep fat for frying	deep fat for frying

Finely chop or mince the chicken and mix with the cream cheese. Add the onion and Parmesan and season with salt and paprika.

Roll the pastry out thinly into a rectangle and cut into 4-inch (10-cm.) squares. Put a spoonful of filling in the centre of each square. Damp the edges and fold over into a triangle. Press the edges firmly together and mark neatly with the back of a fork. Heat the deep fat to 380°F, 190°C (page 18), and fry the kromeskies a few at a time. When they are puffed, golden and risen to the surface, remove from the fat and drain on soft absorbent paper.

Alternative fillings:
Fill each kromesky with a piece of cooked chicken or chicken liver wrapped in streaky bacon, or with the filling for Chicken and ham pie à la Russe (page 22) or Chicken or game piroshki (page 25).

Tomatoes stuffed with chicken and tunny sauce

Serves 6

These stuffed tomatoes make a delicious cold snack. The tomatoes must be firm as well as ripe. If not really large, 2 per portion may be needed.

Imperial	Metric	American
6 large ripe tomatoes	6 large ripe tomatoes	6 large ripe tomatoes
salt and freshly ground pepper	salt and freshly ground pepper	salt and freshly ground pepper
4 oz. cooked chicken, diced	100 g. cooked chicken, diced	$\frac{2}{3}$ cup diced cooked chicken
Tunny fish mayonnaise (page 65)	Tunny fish mayonnaise (page 65)	Tunny fish mayonnaise (page 65)
6 black olives, stoned	6 black olives, stoned	6 ripe olives, pitted

Turn each tomato stem-side downwards and, using a serrated knife, cut off the top. Spoon out all the seeds and core, sprinkle the cases with salt and pepper and turn upside down to drain. Mix the diced chicken with sufficient Tunny fish mayonnaise to bind and fill the tomato cases. Stand them on a serving dish or individual plates. Put the lid back on top of the filling and secure with a cocktail stick topped with a black olive. Garnish with curly endive.

Cold French omelette

Serves 2–3

Imperial	Metric	American
4 eggs	4 eggs	4 eggs
½ oz. butter	15 g. butter	1 tablespoon butter
¼ pint Cheese béchamel sauce (page 60)	1½ dl. Cheese béchamel sauce (page 60)	⅔ cup Cheese béchamel sauce (page 60)
4 oz. cooked chicken or pheasant, diced	100 g. cooked chicken or pheasant, diced	⅔ cup diced cooked chicken or pheasant
1 tablespoon chopped parsley	1 tablespoon chopped parsley	1 tablespoon chopped parsley
1 teaspoon chopped chives or tarragon	1 teaspoon chopped chives or tarragon	1 teaspoon chopped chives or tarragon
salt and pepper	salt and pepper	salt and pepper
watercress for garnish	watercress for garnish	watercress for garnish

Make a large omelette with the eggs and butter in a frying pan. When just cooked, do not fold, but slide out flat on to a large plate and leave to cool.

Mix the sauce with the chicken or pheasant and herbs. Season to taste. Spread this filling over the omelette and roll up. Serve cold garnished with watercress. Accompany with French bread and butter.

Baked savoury potatoes

Serves 4

Baked jacket potatoes are always popular and, with this savoury filling of chicken and mushrooms, make a super supper snack for the garden in summer, or by the fireside in winter.

Imperial	Metric	American
4 large potatoes	4 large potatoes	4 large potatoes
vegetable oil	vegetable oil	vegetable oil
2 oz. mushrooms, sliced	50 g. mushrooms, sliced	½ cup sliced mushrooms
4 oz. butter	100 g. butter	½ cup butter
4 oz. cooked chicken, diced	100 g. cooked chicken, diced	⅔ cup diced cooked chicken
¼ pint soured cream	1½ dl. soured cream	⅔ cup sour cream
1 tablespoon chopped chives	1 tablespoon chopped chives	1 tablespoon chopped chives
salt and black pepper	salt and black pepper	salt and black pepper
3–4 tablespoons milk	3–4 tablespoons milk	4–5 tablespoons milk
4 tablespoons grated cheese	4 tablespoons grated cheese	⅓ cup grated cheese
fresh parsley for garnish	fresh parsley for garnish	fresh parsley for garnish

Scrub the potatoes and halve lengthwise. Brush the cut surface with vegetable oil and place cut side downwards in an oiled baking tray. Prick over the skin with a fork. Bake in a hot oven (400–425°F, 200–220°C, Gas Mark 6–7) for 35–40 minutes or until cooked, according to size.

Meanwhile, fry the mushrooms in 2 tablespoons butter for 3 minutes. Add the chicken, soured cream and chives, heat through. Season with salt and freshly ground black pepper.

Remove the potatoes from the oven and scoop out the pulp. Mash with remaining butter and add sufficient milk to make a creamy consistency. Season with salt and freshly ground pepper. Half fill the potato shells with the potato purée, hollow out the centre. Spoon the chicken mixture into the hollows. Cover with remaining potato, forking it over roughly. Sprinkle with grated cheese and return to the top of the hot oven until golden, or brown under the grill. Garnish with parsley.

Hot chicken mousse with Bercy sauce

Serves 4

This is a tasty light dish to tempt delicate appetites. It is made like a soufflé, but because it is steam-baked it will await the guests' pleasure without collapsing, which makes life easier for many an anxious hostess. A French onion sauce (page 61) may be served instead of the Bercy sauce.

Imperial	Metric	American
10–12 oz. cooked chicken meat	275–350 g. cooked chicken meat	about ¾ lb. cooked chicken meat
oil	oil	oil
2–3 tablespoons crisp breadcrumbs	2–3 tablespoons crisp breadcrumbs	3–4 tablespoons crisp bread crumbs
1 oz. butter	25 g. butter	2 tablespoons butter
1 oz. flour	25 g. flour	¼ cup all-purpose flour
4 tablespoons milk	4 tablespoons milk	⅓ cup milk
4 tablespoons good chicken stock	4 tablespoons good chicken stock	⅓ cup good chicken stock
2 eggs, separated	2 eggs, separated	2 eggs, separated
3 fl. oz. cream	1 dl. cream	6 tablespoons cream
1 tablespoon chopped fresh parsley	1 tablespoon chopped fresh parsley	1 tablespoon chopped fresh parsley
pinch lemon thyme	pinch lemon thyme	pinch lemon thyme
2 teaspoons mushroom or tomato ketchup	2 teaspoons mushroom or tomato ketchup	2 teaspoons mushroom or tomato catsup
salt and freshly ground black pepper	salt and freshly ground black pepper	salt and freshly ground black pepper
about 1 tablespoon lemon juice	about 1 tablespoon lemon juice	about 1 tablespoon lemon juice
½ pint Bercy sauce (page 64)	3 dl. Bercy sauce (page 64)	1¼ cups Bercy sauce (page 64)
fresh lemon and parsley for garnish	fresh lemon and parsley for garnish	fresh lemon and parsley for garnish

Mince the chicken meat very finely.

Oil a cake tin or 1½-pint (1-litre, 3¾-cup) charlotte mould. Put in the crisp crumbs and rotate the tin carefully so that bottom and sides are evenly coated with the crumbs. Turn the tin upside down to tip out any loose surplus crumbs.

Heat the oven to 325–350°F, 170–180°C, Gas Mark 3–4. Make a panada: melt the butter, remove the pan from the heat and blend in the flour and then the milk and the stock. Return to the heat and bring to the simmer, stirring continuously. Cook for 3 minutes into a thick binding sauce.

Mix in the minced chicken. Beat the egg yolks and cream together and stir this into the mixture. Add the parsley, lemon thyme and ketchup. Season well, using plenty of freshly ground black pepper. Sharpen well with lemon juice.

Whisk the whites until stiff, but not brittle. Turn the mixture into a mixing bowl and carefully fold in the egg whites. Pour into the prepared mould and cover with greased paper. Stand the mould in a roasting tin with ½ inch (1 cm.) water in the bottom. Bake for about 1 hour or until set. Test by pressing the top with fingers, it will feel springy when the mousse is ready. Allow to shrink slightly from the sides of the tin, then turn out on to a warm serving dish. Garnish with fresh lemon and parsley and hand Bercy sauce separately or, if preferred, coat with the sauce. Instead of turning it out, the mousse can be cooked and served in a soufflé dish. If made in individual ramekins, they will be cooked in half the time.

Bain-marie or water bath for slow cooking to prevent curdling.

Stuffings for the bird

Almond and chicken liver stuffing

for poussins and small game birds

Imperial	Metric	American
1 chicken liver	1 chicken liver	1 chicken liver
2 oz. rice, boiled	50 g. rice, boiled	scant $\frac{1}{3}$ cup raw rice, boiled
1 oz. ground almonds	25 g. ground almonds	$\frac{1}{4}$ cup ground almonds
4 teaspoons finely chopped onion	4 teaspoons finely chopped onion	4 teaspoons finely chopped onion
4 teaspoons chopped parsley	4 teaspoons chopped parsley	4 teaspoons chopped parsley
pinch basil or majoram	pinch basil or majoram	pinch basil or majoram
salt and freshly ground pepper	salt and freshly ground pepper	salt and freshly ground pepper
2 oz. butter, creamed	50 g. butter, creamed	$\frac{1}{4}$ cup creamed butter
1 egg yolk	1 egg yolk	1 egg yolk

Mash the liver with a fork and mix into the rice with the other dry ingredients and seasonings. Beat in the creamed butter and bind with the egg yolk.

Rice and watercress stuffing

for chicken and game birds

Imperial	Metric	American
2 oz. rice, boiled	50 g. rice, boiled	scant $\frac{1}{3}$ cup raw rice, boiled
1 bunch watercress, finely chopped	1 bunch watercress, finely chopped	1 bunch watercress, finely chopped
2 tablespoons finely chopped celery	2 tablespoons finely chopped celery	3 tablespoons finely chopped celery
1 tablespoon finely chopped onion	1 tablespoon finely chopped onion	1 tablespoon finely chopped onion
1 teaspoon salt	1 teaspoon salt	1 teaspoon salt
freshly ground pepper to taste	freshly ground pepper to taste	freshly ground pepper to taste
1 chicken liver, cleaned	1 chicken liver, cleaned	1 chicken liver, cleaned
2 oz. butter, melted	50 g. butter, melted	$\frac{1}{4}$ cup melted butter
1 small egg, beaten	1 small egg, beaten	1 small egg, beaten

Mix together the drained rice, watercress, celery and onion. Season well with salt and pepper. Chop the chicken liver, or mash with a fork, and stir it into the mixture. Mix in the melted butter and bind with the egg.

Apple, apricot and nut stuffing

for pheasant, guinea fowl and chicken

Imperial	Metric	American
2 oz. cashew nuts	50 g. cashew nuts	⅓ cup cashew nuts
1½ oz. butter	40 g. butter	3 tablespoons butter
3 tablespoons finely chopped celery	3 tablespoons finely chopped celery	scant ¼ cup finely chopped celery
1 tablespoon finely chopped onion	1 tablespoon finely chopped onion	1 tablespoon finely chopped onion
3 oz. apple, cubed	75 g. apple, cubed	½ cup cubed apple
2 oz. white bread, diced	50 g. white bread, diced	1 cup diced white bread
3 oz. dried apricots, chopped	75 g. dried apricots, chopped	½ cup chopped dried apricots
½ teaspoon dried savory or rosemary	½ teaspoon dried savory or rosemary	½ teaspoon dried savory or rosemary
salt, pepper and lemon juice to taste	salt, pepper and lemon juice to taste	salt, pepper and lemon juice to taste

Chop the nuts coarsely. Melt the butter in a small saucepan and fry the nuts until just colouring. Add the celery, onion and apple, fry gently until slightly softened. Mix in the bread, apricots, herbs and seasoning. Stir until well mashed together. Sharpen to taste with lemon juice.

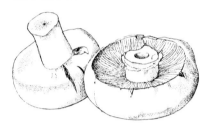

Farce for galantine of chicken

Imperial	Metric	American
8 oz. lean pork, minced	225 g. lean pork, minced	1 cup ground lean pork
4 oz. veal, minced	100 g. veal, minced	½ cup ground veal
4 oz. ham, chopped	100 g. ham, chopped	½ cup chopped cooked ham
4 oz. button mushrooms, chopped	100 g. button mushrooms, chopped	1 cup chopped button mushrooms
1 chicken liver	1 chicken liver	1 chicken liver
1 oz. butter	25 g. butter	2 tablespoons butter
1–2 tablespoons brandy	1–2 tablespoons brandy	1–3 tablespoons brandy
2 shallots or button onions, chopped, or 1 clove garlic, chopped	2 shallots or button onions, chopped, or 1 clove garlic, chopped	2 shallots or tiny onions, chopped, or 1 clove garlic, chopped
1 tablespoon chopped parsley	1 tablespoon chopped parsley	1 tablespoon chopped parsley
grated rind ½ lemon	grated rind ½ lemon	grated rind ½ lemon
salt and freshly ground black pepper	salt and freshly ground black pepper	salt and freshly ground black pepper
1 egg, beaten	1 egg, beaten	1 egg, beaten

Work together the pork, veal, ham and mushrooms. Clean the chicken liver and fry in the hot butter for a few minutes until stiffened. Chop and add to the minced meat. Pour the brandy into the frying pan, boil up and add to the farce. Add the onion or garlic, parsley and lemon rind. Season well with salt and pepper. Mix thoroughly and bind with the beaten egg.

Preparation and serving suggestions

To make hot French garlic bread

Slash a long French loaf across in slices 1–1¼ inches (2½–3 cm.) wide, without cutting right through. Mash a large clove of pressed garlic into 4 oz. (100 g., ½ cup) softened butter. Spread mixture generously between the slices. Wrap the loaf in aluminium foil and bake in a hot oven (400°F, 200°C, Gas Mark 6) for about 10 minutes.

The preparation and cleaning of mussels

Throughout cleaning, keep mussels in cold water. Discard any with broken shells, any that are gaping open and any in which the 2 shells can be slid against each other—the latter will be full of sand and make the others gritty. With a sharp knife, remove the beard or seaweed-like bits protruding from the shell, scrape off any barnacles or limpets. Scrub the shells and wash them in several waters until finally the water comes out quite free from grit.

Vegetable recipe suggestions

Corn on the cob Indian style: Turn back the husks and strip off the silky threads. Fold back the husks again so the kernel is covered by the leaves and roast over a charcoal brazier, turning frequently, for 15–20 minutes. To serve, remove husks, spread corn with butter and serve with salt and ground pepper.

Corn fritters: Add 6 tablespoons of self-raising flour to 1 (8 oz., 225 g.) can corn kernels and mix in 2 beaten eggs. Heat butter in a frying pan and drop the batter in by the tablespoonful. Fry until golden brown, turn and fry on other side. Serve immediately.

Courgettes au gratin: Wipe the courgettes, remove stalks and halve lengthwise. In a shallow flameproof casserole, fry the cut surfaces in hot butter. Turn over, season well and sprinkle with grated Parmesan cheese. Cover and bake in a moderate oven (350°F, 180°C, Gas Mark 4) for 20–30 minutes according to size. When serving, pour over a little warmed cream.

Jacket potatoes: Prick the potatoes and brush with oil. Bake in a hot oven (425°F, 220°C, Gas Mark 7) for 1 hour or longer, according to size. When cooked, cut a cross in the top, squeeze up the fluff and fork in parsley butter, soured cream and chopped chives or crispy bacon bits. Serve in folded coloured napkins.

Spinach croquettes: Add 2 oz. (50 g., ½ cup) grated Parmesan cheese to 12 oz. (350 g.) cooked, drained and chopped spinach. Season with nutmeg, salt and pepper and beat in 2 egg yolks. Form the mixture into small croquettes on a floured board. Roll them in breadcrumbs and fry in hot oil or butter.

Index